YUKON
CHALLENGE

YUKON CHALLENGE

JOHN FIRTH

LONE
PINE

The Publishers:
Lone Pine Publishing
206, 10426 - 81st Avenue
Edmonton, Alberta
T6E 1X5

Canadian Cataloguing in Publication Data
Firth, John, 1953-
    Yukon challenge

    ISBN 0-919433-85-5

    1. Yukon Quest International Sled Dog Race.
2. Sled dog racing—Yukon Territory—History
I. Title.
SF440.15.F57 1990   798'.8'097191   C91-091048-0

Cover and layout design: Beata Kurpinski
Cover illustration: Horst Krause
Mapping: Rick Checkland
Editorial: Gary Whyte
Printing: Gagné Printing, Louiseville, Québec, Canada

The publisher gratefully acknowledges the assistance of the Federal Department of Communications, Alberta Culture and Multiculturalism, the Canada Council, the Recreation, Parks and Wildlife Foundation, and the Alberta Foundation for the Literary Arts in the publication of this book.

The Yukon Quest is the result of years of

dedication from the founders of the race.

It is the reward for the volunteers who put in

endless hours during the most bitter months of the year.

It is the ultimate symbol of what it means to be a dog driver.

It is the supreme achievement for the true

athletes of this event, the dogs.

This book is dedicated to all of them.

CONTENTS

ACKNOWLEDGEMENTS

Like the Yukon Quest itself, the bottom line of this book is contributions, moral and material; those who contributed are the recipients of my deepest appreciation for their assistance:

Laura Louise Chapman for telling me to stop thinking about writing this story and do something about it. Roger Williams, Jocelyn Williams and Leroy Shank for being so enthusiastic and contributing so much to the success of my work in Fairbanks. Bob Eley, for late nights at the Fairbanks Daily News Miner.

Frenchy De Rushé, for allowing a total stranger he has never met to use his poem. Jackie Pierce, for long Saturday afternoons at the Whitehorse Star and for use of the Star's extensive photo files for this book. All photographs in the book are used by permission of the Whitehorse Star. I would especially thank Yukon Quest International for their permission to reprint the 1988 Race Rules.

Dave Monson, Bill Cotter, Kathy Swenson, Sonny Lindner, Joe Runyan, Harry and Sandy Sutherland, Jon Rudolph, Frank Turner, Lorrina and Gordie Mitchell, Ralph and Shari Tingey, Senley Yuill, Hans Oettli, Jim Reiter and Lou and Carol Johnson for sharing their insight and experience. Jackie Parsons and Janice Drake for their typing from dictation skills. Shane Horsnell for his computer skills. Dawn Dimond for on-the-spot feedback and tolerance when there were papers spread out everywhere. Mary Walters Riskin, Jane Spalding and Grant Kennedy at Lone Pine for the direction that put me on the road to literary immortality.

There are many other people who have also, over the past five years supplied me with information and support even though they may have been totally unaware of it. And there will be those we inevitably forget to make note of at the time and leave out of the list of thank yous. Without their invaluable assistance this book would never have been written.

THE YUKON QUEST

The Yukon Quest is a measured test
Of man and dog versus trail
But more than that it's a satement
Of the strong will not to fail.

Where the musher stands, not against the land
But against unspoken fear...
The bitter cold and the loneliness
And silence that hurts to hear!

The Quest is more than finishing first,
It's more than how slow or how fast;
It's a thousand miles on the winter trail,
Where a winner may finish last.

The men and the women who live for the trail,
For the huskies' lonesome call,
And the bone weary camps at the end of the day;
They'd sell their souls for it all!

They love, and they live it and 12 months each year
They give it their very best,
And they dream of the long lonesome trail ahead,
Once again on the Yukon Quest.

W.M. Frenchy De Rushé
1986

INTRODUCTION

This is not just a story about a race. It is more a book about the kind of people who would conceive of such an event, the individuals who would take part in it and the dogs that make it a reality. The driving of dogs — it is as much a philosophy of life as it is a necessary means of transportation or a recreational pastime. The romantic fantasies of pioneers in search of adventure, glory and wealth that were first publicized by Jack London, Robert Service and television's Sergeant Preston and his dog King: these are the idealistic images that lured many who now populate Alaska and the Yukon.

They portrayed an unforgiving world of deceptive beauty and ruthless winter; a land of environmental contradictions where the sun shone at midnight, the moon waxed at noon and the silent shroud of night was ripped by dancing lights and crackling music of unknown origin.

It was an eerie world that could only be conquered by dogs blessed with undying loyalty, unburdened affection, limitless endurance and quick intelligence. Behind them, riding sled runners and inspiring the dogs to even greater heights of accomplishment, were their drivers: the strong who somehow found a way to survive where the weak perished. There were men and women of stout heart and childlike innocence who triumphed through sheer intestinal fortitude and the gritty determination to succeed at any price. They endured the pain and loneliness of the trail to find comfort in the camaraderie of others who shared the same hardships.

It was the desire to find within themselves that romantic fantasy and the pioneer spirit that drove a few modern northerners into the world of driving dogs. Some believe that the dog drivers, or mushers, are the only genuine northerners left; that everyone else, with their creature comforts, has compromised with nature or hidden from it rather than confronting it head-on.

Some drivers hitch up dogs through necessity. Dogs and sleds are more reliable than gasoline-powered snow machines for moving supplies, freight and mail to isolated communities and cabins in the dead of winter.

Others set foot on the runners for adventure. They simply enjoy the satisfaction of merging with the wilderness, traversing virgin country and developing the skills that form the foundation of arctic survival.

Occasionally the drivers would meet on a trail and it was always fun to race just to see who was the fastest. It was only a matter of time before their fun got serious and drivers started pitting themselves against each other, against a clock and against the environment.

The measured courses got longer and longer, from short 15-mile sprint tracks, to middle-distance 400 mile events until one day the drivers strove to surpass the magical figure of 1000 miles in a single race.

In this era of space shuttles and jet planes carrying people around the world in a few hours, or satellite communications sending messages across continents in seconds, we tend to forget just how far 1000 miles is or exactly what kind of an effort is required to travel it.

At one time, people and messages could only travel by horseback, stagecoach, on foot or by dog sled. What takes us a few hours or a few seconds to do today, used to take weeks, sometimes months or years, to complete. And this compression of time and effort hasn't taken hundreds of years to achieve. It has occurred entirely within the confines of the twentieth century.

To earn some appreciation of this phenomenon, next time you commute from your home to work, leave the car at home or save your bus fare and walk to your place of employment. Don't pick a nice sunny, warm day to do it. Try a blustery, cold day with some rain or sleet. If you haven't had the opportunity to wade knee-deep in snow, try walking along a beach with your shins immersed in the surf.

Then think about what it would be like to do that 24 hours a day for two weeks — not because you have to do it, but because you want to. That's what the Yukon Quest is like.

This book follows the 1988 Yukon Quest for two reasons. First, the 1988 race runs in the direction that was followed when the race was first run in 1984 (it is run in the opposite direction on alternate years). And, second, it was a classic confrontation, possibly the last of its kind, between the best of the new scientific dog mushers and one of the great drivers of the old traditional school of hard knocks.

There were four races prior to the 1988 race, and these will be referred to in the book. And there have been two races since which will also be talked about. Each of them had their highlights and no two were alike. There will be many more Yukon Quests, many more champions and many more experiences which can only be documented by some future writer. But the essence of the event will never change and that is what this book is about.

Route of the Yukon Quest

ALASKA

Central Circle
Angel Creek
Fairbanks   Circle Eagle
Hot   Dawson
Springs

YUKON

N.W.T.

Carmacks
Whitehorse

B.C.

February 20, 1988
In the night, the day begins to change.

Just before warm weather turns to cold, there's a crispness in the air you can smell. Maybe it's the drop in the humidity or the increased density of the environment. Whatever the source of the tang, once you've tasted it and know what it heralds, it's something you can never forget.

It doesn't tell you if it's going to snow, or whether there will be winds, or how cold it will get. It is simply one of nature's ways of letting you know there is a change on the way. This night you can smell it; tomorrow will be cold.

A mass of Arctic air is rolling in. Sometime this afternoon the weather front is due to arrive over Fairbanks. Fresh snow and high winds will precede it; then the Alaskan interior will be locked in a deep-freeze. The mercury, already starting to drop, will finally stabilize reluctantly around minus 50 degrees.

And it's going to stay around for a while. The city of 60,000 is going to be forced to deal with cars too frozen to start and roads barricaded by drifting snow well into next week.

Huddled in a small second-floor office, protected from the night air by groaning hot water heaters, Yukon Quest race manager Jack Niggemyer is listening to the weather forecast with only half an ear.

He isn't too concerned about what the weather will be later today or tomorrow. He will still have to do what is necessary to ensure the success of the race, regardless of snow, cold and wind. On his shoulders rides the ultimate responsibility of making sure there's a trail to follow to the Canadian border and that the checkpoints en route are staffed.

Once the racers are across the boundary, his job is finished. At that point his Canadian counterpart, the tall white-bearded Art Christensen, from Whitehorse, Yukon, takes over.

As the greys of dawn replace the dark of night outside his downtown office window, he heaves a sigh of aggravation through his untrimmed black goatee.

There is a multitude of last minute emergencies covering his desk in paper and clogging his telephone lines. The outer offices and the Yukon Quest board room are filled with volunteers trying to resolve other hassles or to organize the starting line personnel.

A block north of him, on the Chena River, one problem can't be solved on paper or by phone. Unseasonably warm temperatures over the past two weeks have left the ice under the starting chute thinner than Niggemyer likes. It will probably support the teams and officials without buckling, but if the crowd of "mush- aholics" who want to get too close to the action becomes too big, there is the potential of disaster.

"The thing is," he says to the enquiring media crowded around the door to his office, "we're afraid the ice is in grave danger of collapsing if too many people stand on it."

He has been broadcasting that message, over the air and in print, for the past few days. The alternative, he has been saying, is to watch the start from the Chena River Bridge or the river bank. But Niggemyer knows that telling people is one thing. Whether or not they listen is another.

Three Quest volunteers, Bob Goodwin, Randy Navin and Joe Calvin, are oblivious to the thin ice. In the early morning dusk, they are drilling holes in the ice in which they will set the 20-foot-tall posts that support the yellow and red Yukon Quest Start banner over the center of the river. Around them stand the 45-gallon gas drums filled with water that act as fence posts. Wired to the gas drums is the snow fencing used to hold back the crowd.

A hundred yards behind, up on the riverbank just past the bridge, the parking lot behind the Fairbanks North Star Borough administration building (city hall) is starting to look surprisingly busy for a Saturday morning. But cars and trucks form the minority of the parking stall occupants on this day.

A dog lot and the starting chute of a long distance race have to be seen to be believed. Kimberley Sessions, from Atlanta, Georgia, arrived in Fairbanks just yesterday to visit a friend. She has never seen a sled dog or a dog sled much less a dog race of this nature.

Crammed in the crowd on the Chena River Bridge, kept warm by the closeness of the other bodies around her, she thinks about how different it is back home. The winter. The people. And above all, the dogs. This reality vastly exceeds the fantasy.

"I'm amazed. My whole vision of the north was Jack London. White Fang and that kind of stuff. This was by far the most exciting thing I've ever seen."

Six hundred dogs are chained to the sides of vehicles or to cables stretched out across the ground. Or they are sticking their heads out of windows in the dog boxes on the backs of pick-ups and small trucks.

Inside their little cubby-hole, the dogs have enough room to stand, curl up and sleep or stretch out on their straw beds. But the comforts of their boxes are the last thing on their minds now. The activity all around tells them this is the place and now is the time to RUN.

The parking lot is barely large enough to contain the mass of animals, men and machines. Inside that space there are several confusing unspoken signals being sent between drivers, the dogs are being affected by being in close proximity with each other, and there is a tremendous concentration of frustrated and anxious energy from both drivers and teams.

Their howling and barking and the meaty-smelling clouds of their breath thicken the air. They strain at their chains, crouch and yowl with excitement or bound frantically into the air. All the time they are emptying their bladders and bowels. Some of them are digging up the frozen earth turning the snow into a brownish slop.

18

In this canine-dominated world gone crazy, the dog mushers move confidently and quietly in the eyes of their hurricanes. They and their handlers wander unruffled through the bedlam carrying bags of dog food, sleeping bags, camp stoves, and boxes and bags of unknown content.

Among the mushers there is a housewife, two lawyers, a sports promoter, an author, a dentist, a few fishermen, an artist, some carpenters, a retired cattle rancher and his two sons, heavy equipment operators, the owner of a highway lodge, several trappers, a grandmother and those who claim to have no profession at all or don't know what they do.

They come from Great Britain, Alaska, Illinois, Washington, France, the Yukon and British Columbia. Their homes are located in heavily populated metropolitan cores, in small towns, in villages that don't even get a dot on the map or on the banks of lakes and rivers miles from their nearest neighbour. There are five women and 42 men. The youngest is 21. The oldest is 58. Two have listed their ages as "unknown" and "forgotten."

They have only one thing in common: they all drive dogs.

Bill Cotter stands almost lost in the milling bystanders. The building contractor from Nenana, Alaska, isn't the kind of person who wants to stand out in a crowd. It was his ability to achieve that effect that won him the 1987 Yukon Quest championship.

His smile is shy. His eyes are deceptively soft. His voice barely climbs above a whisper. But there is a competitors intensity about him. Even though he is not running this year, he still feels the starting line edge. Like the other drivers around him, he shows no reaction at the news of the encroaching Arctic front.

"It's just one of the things we live with. Nothing else exists for you except the race. Your focus is narrowed down to one thing. The world economy, war, drought in the mid-west: that has no meaning. The only thing that's important is your dog team, yourself, the environment around you, keeping your dogs and yourself healthy. Survival.

I think the hardships we take for granted would kill most people. We almost look forward to the prospect of those hardships because we've adapted ourselves to deal with those circumstances."

A lot of the mushers don't even hear the weather report, but they know what's coming. They can smell it. Besides that, their dogs stopped shedding their excess fur a day or so ago, indicating they will still have need of their winter coats.

Each driver who stands in this parking lot today, who has stood in it in the past or will stand in it in the future, has his or her own reason for being there.

Kathy Swenson measures you with every glance. In this world of strategy and deception, this slightly built mother of two has learned not to take anything at face value at first sight. Her husband Rick, four-time winner of the Iditarod[1], is a master of the head games that mushers play and some of his ability has rubbed off on her. But along with the acquired knowledge comes the pressure of being the wife of Rick Swenson.

"If I changed my name, it would be different," says the woman who had to adapt to the Alaska winter after being raised in the Florida sun, "But I'm Swenson. I'm expected to have a strong team and I'm expected to do well."

Learning to cope with pressure didn't come easy though. Swenson's first long distance race was the 1986 Quest. For the first three days, she was unable to eat. "I was in shock. But I finally relaxed and settled down."

She finished that race in 17th place. In 1987, she became the first woman to finish in the top ten - fourth overall, less than an hour behind Cotter. For anyone else, that might have been enough. But she is a Swenson: she feels she can do better. Kathy Swenson intends to win.

Bob Bright is better known as a sports promoter in Chicago, Illinois, but he's also a winter regular on the Alaskan sled dog racing circuit.

"It's a great adventure. Where else can you go and spend days on the back of a dog sled looking at some of the most beautiful country in the world?"

His technique for combatting the cold and fatigue he faces on the trail is making sure he has the proper diet. Into his high-tech titanium sled he packs deep-dish pizzas and pork chops donated by a restaurant owned by another sporting personality, Chicago Bears coach Mike Ditka. On top sits chili and chinese food.

"I tell you something. You get pretty damned hungry out there, especially in this kind of climate, if you don't have food you like to eat."

The trail philosopher is the diminutive Frank Turner who lives alone in a cabin on the banks of the Pelly River in the Yukon. Or almost alone. He shares his homestead with 30 dogs. The bespectacled sage claims he discovered he had a genetic pre- disposition

20

towards dog mushing 16 years ago when he stepped in a pile of dog poop and didn't mind the smell. He is also one of only two drivers who have competed in every Yukon Quest.

Zen and motorcycle maintenance doesn't hold a candle to existentialism and dog mushing. He savours the bitter cold and hardship of his lifestyle. "I have such a heightened sense of being alive. There's so much exhiliration. I can still enjoy mushing, I haven't lost it. If I ever do, it'll be time to move onto sailing or even tiddly-winks."

He adjusts his eyeglasses, then gazes thoughtfully at his team which stares expectantly back. They may not be aware of it, but Turner is graduating up one level in his own personal Yukon Quest. Rather than running the race just for the experience, this year he is raising funds for the Yukon Association for Special Needs People: an organization that works with the physically and mentally handicapped.

"I'm using the race as a vehicle for things beyond the race. It's a sense of giving something back somehow. I've always looked at the Quest from the beginning as being a number of levels, and this is one of the levels: to do something."

Ed Borden was here in 1986. A chemist from Kenai, Alaska, he wasn't here to win. Nor was he here simply for the experience of driving a long distance race. He had two Iditarod races under his belt already. He was there because he had to do it while he could. Borden suffers from Multiple Sclerosis: a disease that may never affect his life or could permanently disable him. Borden was determined to make the most of what he had while he had it.

William Kleedehn will have two things to demonstrate when he steps into this hallowed ground in 1990. He will be determined to show that just because he has only one leg, he isn't any more handicapped on the trail than anyone else. And second, he will want to see if, as a musher from the east (Kenora, Ontario), he can compete with the driving elite of Alaska.

In 1989, Jennine Cathers will make her mark in Quest history. She will be half of the first daughter-father team to enter the race (along with her father Ned, who is in this parking lot in 1988 preparing for his first attempt). The tall teenager with the fashion model features desires to be the youngest musher to ever enter, compete and finish: her 18th birthday, the minimum age allowed to compete, will fall on the closing day for entries that year.

Two nights before this parking lot bedlam, the order of departure had been determined at the starting banquet where the drivers drank beer, ate food, listened to speeches and pulled numbers out of a fur hat.

Now the announcers at the start line are calling for the first sled. Jerry Riley had lifted out number one from the hat. He heads his team out of the parking lot, over the riverbank and along the ice to the starting banner.

Considered one of the toughest drivers on the racing circuit, the stocky 55-year-old commercial fisherman, who won the 1976 Iditarod, is also one of the old school of mushing. While others have moved to specific breeding programs, high powered food and specialized equipment, he has continued to raise dogs the way he did while growing up in his home village in the Alaskan Interior.

"I use dry dog food and give them their shots. That's high tech for me."

The Alaskan Native is also considered one of the masters of subterfuge on the trail. Other drivers know it's what Riley isn't saying or doing that's important. He never really does not tell the truth about himself and his team, it just sort of comes out like a half truth. The problem is figuring out which half to believe — and when to believe it.

"You run into Gerry in the summer and he tells you about his back and how bad it is. His dogs are sick; worse than that, they're dying. He doesn't know if he's going to race this year or not," smiles Jon Gleason, "The next time you see him, in the race, you're looking at his bad back and his dying dogs leave you in the dust."

Gleason, a former professional motorcycle racer who gave up the wheels in favour of dog mushing, will follow close behind Riley. He watches Riley pull out of the parking lot, then returns to preparing his team to start his third Yukon Quest.

As Riley draws up to the starting chute, volunteers and officials step forward to assist him. It's not easy. The dogs yelp, leap and drive towards the trail ahead of them. Three or four people hang onto the neck lines, restraining them. A half dozen more anchor down the sled.

Riley walks down the team, rubbing each dog on the head, talking quietly to them, reminding them who is boss. It is like watching a coach preparing his team for the big game: trying to

Last minute consultation between lead dog and Jeff King, 1988.

calm them down yet keep them pumped up. But there is more of a relationship between the musher and his dogs, bordering on something like a parent-child bond rather than just players and their mentor.

He turns and responds to a question or statement from the people crowded up against the snow fence. Most of the spectators have listened to Niggemyer's warnings and are watching from the bridge behind the starting chute, or from the riverbank. A few of those who venture onto the ice pay the price later in the morning when they drop through into ice-cold ankle-deep water near the shore line.

Somebody shouts at Riley from near the announcer's booth. He looks back at the sled, at the dogs, down the trial, then jogs back to his sled. The starter's flag goes up. The timer counts down.

"Three.

Two.

One.

Go!"

The flag drops, the volunteers fall back and the team surges forward. Riley rides with all his weight holding down his brake

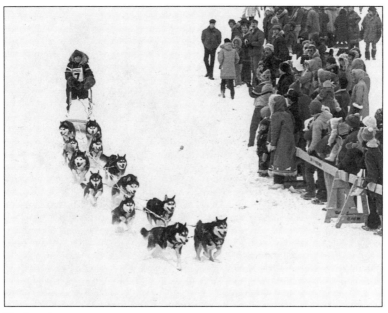

The Race is on.

through the starting area; not until he is past the crowd does he step off the brake and let the dogs have their head.

Others carry passengers for extra weight; some drag an anchor, which can be anything from another sled to an old rubber tire, behind themselves: anything to slow down the teams who are fresh, strong and pumped up with the sheer joy of finally being let loose to run. All the frustrations and confusion of the parking lot are left behind in this initial burst for freedom on the trail.

At this point, the driver's job is simply to hang onto the sled and try not to let the dogs get out of control. Too much speed now could result in injury to driver or dogs or could damage the sled. In addition, an out-of-control sled whipping through spectators can be dangerous. The passenger or anchor will be dropped off or cut loose once the sled passes beyond the crowds.

Behind him, in their predetermined order, the rest of the competitors file down from the parking lot in two minute intervals. Forty-seven times the starting chute sequence is repeated. The barking and yowling of dogs diminish as the teams leave. Then, finally, there is silence. The crowd pauses for a moment, reluctant to leave, then they gradually start to drift away from the Chena

24

Pecos Humphries making history, first musher to ever start, 1984.

River. Now they must rely on the media to know what's happening out there on the trail.

Lawyer-turned-professional dog musher Dave Monson is the thirteenth driver to pull out from the starting chute. The superstition surrounding the number doesn't bother him. One of the pre-race favorites, the second-place finisher of the 1987 Quest is, in fact, quite delighted with it. The number thirteen is considered a good omen in the Iditarod — a race that Monson's wife Susan Butcher has already won twice — and he is planning to make it lucky in this race also.

A few minutes behind him is Rick Atkinson, the stubbornly dogged Scotsman who tried to steal the 1985 race but faltered in the home stretch. A documentary film about his second-place finish that year has won several major international awards. The veteran of dog driving in Antarctica is at his best in the wilderness and 16 years of experience as a mountaineering guide cannot be discounted.

Then Jeff King sets off: another pre-race favorite, with his intense gaze that reflects a single-minded determination to win. A construction contractor, he is the only musher other than Turner to have raced in all the Yukon Quests so far. He has been in the thick of the fight every time but has fallen short in every race to now. The smart money rides on his sled this year. He is due.

"Pecos" Humphries, the long-bearded trapper from Talkeetna, Alaska, was the first musher to start the inaugural Quest in 1984. The luck of the draw at the musher's banquet that year gave him a claim to fame that no one else can ever take away.

"Maybe I'll be a trivia question 10 years from now," mused Humphries, who came north for a short stint with the United States Air Force in 1973 and just never left .

Former Iowa rodeo rider and artist Jim Reiter sweats over whether or not he has covered all his bases. In addition to the approximately $10,000 in cash each driver invests, there is a lot of physical and emotional preparation for the race. But, at the start line, what is left undone remains undone. What is forgotten , stays forgotten, and stays behind. Most of the time.

In this case, what Reiter has forgotten doesn't get left behind when he kicks off to help the dogs break the runners from the snow . . . it goes with him. In his pocket is the key to his truck and left stranded at the start line is his girlfriend and handler Debbie Styer. Undaunted, she starts looking for a ride to Angel Creek, the first checkpoint 75 miles away.

Ahead of the teams lies the Yukon Quest Trail: one thousand miles of a narrow one-way track cut in the snow across three major mountain ranges, through miles of thick underbrush and trees and down much of the length of the Yukon, one of North America's great rivers.

The route to Angel Creek is, comparatively speaking, the easiest leg of the entire race, but it also can trap the unwary. The track meanders along the Chena River for about 15 miles. The ice is fairly smooth, most of it covered by a crust of snow. Other areas have been swept clear by the winds exposing glare ice: a surface on which the dogs can find no secure footing and which is highly reflective, often preventing the driver from seeing any hazardous features.

The trail then turns off the river, following smaller streams and bush trails. Twisting and winding through the trees, it occasionally emerges to run parallel to the Chena Hot Springs Road before dropping onto the north fork of the Chena River which takes it to Angel Creek.

This is a land greatly transformed since Jack McQuesten drove his dogs into the Tanana River in the winter of 1878 to trade for furs. That was the first recorded trip by a white man into what was then virgin country and is now criss-crossed by hundreds of winter dog sled and snow machine trails.

The marked Quest trail was primarily a freighting trail and mail route in the early part of the twentieth century. It was also the route along which Juchiro Wada, a Japanese cook and renowned long distance musher in the 1890s, started out into the ice fog and minus 50 degree temperatures to carry word of the 1902 gold strike.

That journey almost ended Wada's life: not because of the hardships he faced on the trail, but because when the stampeders arrived, they found there was lots of gold but no food to get them through the winter.

They decided at first to lynch the cook, then trading post owner, E.T. Barnette, was ultimately fingered as the culprit. Barnette sold them all his food at cut rate prices, then temporarily skipped town on the next dog sled heading north along this same track. Wada, his neck-tie party cancelled by Barnette's flight, survived to mush again.

The shortest Yukon Quest ever run ended in 1986 just 20 miles from Fairbanks.

Ralph Nestor was running alongside his sled when the trail took a sharp turn to the left. The dogs made the corner and so did the sled. But Nestor was slingshotted away from the sled and kept going in a straight line, colliding head- first with a tree. He stood up. His legs seemed a little shaky and he had a minor amount of dizziness.

"I'll just take a bit of a break," he muttered to himself, "Then I'll keep on going." Dentist and dog driver Ron Rosser was right behind Nestor. He glanced at Nestor's head. "I don't think you should keep going," he suggested to Nestor, "I can see your skull through your hair."

Nestor put his hand to his head where it landed on a cold, smooth surface. He pulled down his hand and looked at it, but there was only a little blood. Most of it had frozen on the exposed bone.

Rosser loaded the injured musher on his sled and carried him a couple of miles to the highway. A motorist took him to Fairbanks Memorial Hospital. Nestor's Quest ended with a black eye, 72 stitches, a place in the record books and a new lesson for his students when he returned to his job — he is the director of the travel industry management program at the University of Alaska in Fairbanks.

It is getting close to dusk when nature calls Lorrina Mitchell. At first she figures she can ignore it, but it won't go away.

"Now this is not usually a problem in the summertime, but when you're wearing all your layers of clothes, it requires a lot more preparation . . . to find a convenient place to secure the team and to make sure you don't have too much company on the trail."

She picks her spot, put the snow hook around a tree then, almost as an afterthought, ties another rope to another tree.

The first woman to have ever finished the Yukon Quest, 11th place in 1984, she grew up surrounded by dog drivers in the northern British Columbia bush. Even her love life has been connected with mushing.

A romantic dog sled ride to an isolated cabin for the weekend was supposed to be the ultimate experience for Mitchell and her boyfriend a few years ago. The weekend turned somewhat less than romantic when the sled tipped over and the boyfriend was knocked out. Mitchell had to load him into the sled and spent the weekend trying to cure his headache. It may not have gone as planned, but the romance continued. The boyfriend was Gordie Mitchell, now her husband and handler.

Two days before the race she had put on her most alluring black evening dress and cranked up her most feminine charms for the mushers' banquet because "as of Saturday, you can't tell the girls from the boys, so tonight we're helping you out." As she wrestles with her clothes in the trees, she thinks about how much easier this might be if she was a boy.

A few moments later, her pants down around her knees, her heart isn't the only thing that comes to a halt as she hears her team start heading off down the trail. The snow hook bounces loose, but the extra snub-line, the one she tied as an afterthought, holds. She recovers her pants, her composure and her team and spends the rest of the day wondering how she would have explained this one if that extra rope hadn't held.

There is a steep embankment to scale as the drivers turn off the Chena River and into the bush. Ed Salter, one of Alaska's premiere sled dog builders, got hung up on this escarpment in 1987. His lead dogs were over the top but for some reason the team didn't want to pull the sled up. Jon Gleason gave him a hand to finish the climb, then his team started up the hill and stopped in exactly the same position.

"Dogs can be so stupid sometimes," sums up Gleason, "It's almost like it was written, 'you will get to the top and you will stop and you will not go any further no matter how much they cuss and swear.' At that particular point, all our dogs have got the same damn name: you dumb sonofabitch. I don't care whose team it is, we've all got the same dumb dogs and they all have the same name."

Getting lost is not uncommon on this part of the trail. With so many tracks cutting across the race route, a wrong turn or a missed marker is expected. Mushers often find themselves knocking on cabin doors to ask directions or sitting in gravel pits with one set of sled runner marks, their own, entering and none going out. Most often, the solution is backtracking to find out where the mistake was made. Providing you don't make another error while backtracking, it usually works. Sometimes it's sheer luck or divine providence that provides the solution.

Harry Sutherland, a wirey ex-paratrooper turned carpenter-dog driver, prayed he would find the trail soon in 1986 after taking a wrong turn and, sure enough, his inspiration came from above. "I was really disoriented. I turned around. I went across a gravel pit and into the woods. I was stumbling around and pretty soon a helicopter comes over and there are a couple of TV guys from Fairbanks in it. I've got to talk to those guys. Get them to land. I'm waving at them and they come down." Sutherland's weathered face has wrinkles in it when he's relaxed. When he's angry or frustrated, the wrinkles turn into gullies. The journalists could see that Sutherland was upset. When he started running again, the helicopter hovered overhead, the reporters pointing the way back to the trail.

The first one to arrive at Angel Creek in 1988 isn't an official, a dog or a driver. As Steve and Ann Verbanec, owners of the popular weekend bar that serves as the first checkpoint, prepare for the onslaught of spectators, media, organizers, and volunteers, a small moose strolls casually into the parking lot and stands watching all the commotion.

After a few minutes it wanders over to warm itself by a campfire on the edge of the yard. Eventually, with no musher in sight yet and bored with being gawked at, the moose saunters back into the trees and disappears.

There are two schools of thought about arriving first at the first checkpoint. It may be an advantage, providing a small psychological lift similar to the kind of boost a sprinter gets when he knows he's had a good start. Or it may be a disadvantage to have a lead at this early stage because of the feeling you get having all those other teams following along behind you, taking advantage of the work you did breaking trail.

"Dogs that go out after number one can really move it without using up a lot of energy because they chase the leading teams like a fox chases rabbits," says Pecos Humphries.

Never one to hang back and let someone else set the pace, Jeff King is the first to arrive in the late evening darkness. For King, his moustache and fur trim around his parka hood hanging with icicles, being first into Angel Creek is an analytical satisfaction. It gives him the opportunity to take a better look at Kathy Swenson and David Monson than they will get at him.

King's stoic reaction at reaching the first checkpoint contrasts strongly with the euphoric high that Stan Bearup felt when he arrived in 1985. Bearup was in the middle of the pack, but for the resident of North Pole, Alaska, his position in the standings wasn't that important. The fact that he had even gotten this far was reason enough to celebrate. A year earlier the young Native from North Pole, Alaska, had almost died while training for the Quest.

A burst blood vessel in his brain, suffered while he was out in the bush running his dogs, almost killed him. Another musher came across him lying on the trail and carried him to help. "You'll be partially paralysed for the rest of your life," his doctors informed him, "Forget about the Quest. You're going to have enough trouble just walking."

Medically they may have been right, but doctors are also aware that special events or specific goals can cause people to accomplish the impossible with their health, even to the extent of cheating death. And, like most Alaskans, Bearup hated to be told he couldn't do something that he wanted to.

The training started the day he left the hospital. His 1984 Christmas present to himself was officially filing his entry papers. When he stepped off the sled at the first checkpoint, he crossed over a psychological barrier just as great as the physical one he was on his way to conquering. A few days later he completed the race he was told he could never run.

Angel Creek Lodge was a lay-over spot on the old winter road between Fairbanks and the Circle District. Today the weather-worn log structure is home for a bevy of outdoor winter activities such as snow-mobile sprints and middle-distance and sprint dog sled races and indoor activities like Trivial Pursuit tournaments. It didn't actually become an official checkpoint for the Yukon Quest until 1986.

For two years the Quest trail simply ran past the front door to Chena Hot Springs, 15 miles further up the valley. The hospitality at Chena was fine, but the environment left a lot to be desired.

The warm ground around the thermal springs resort kept the snow in a perpetual state of slush: half water, half snow. The dogs would rest in the slush and be soaking wet when it was time to go. The water would freeze in the fur once they left the warmth, depriving the dogs of their natural insulation against the cold. The mushers also didn't like the idea of giving mineralized water to their teams. Anything out of the ordinary introduced into their diet at this stage could make the entire team sick and end their race right there.

So the decision was made by organizers to move the check-point to Angel Creek. There is lots of room for the drivers to park their teams outside the lodge and the Verbanecs keep three large barrels of fresh, unmineralized water warming near a fire. Check-point life for the dogs has improved, but the mushers are the ones who pay the price. Angel Creek isn't what the drivers consider a peaceful checkpoint. Most of the spectators crowd into the bar at the lodge, which is the only place the mushers can rest.

They get a good meal here: stew, some pasta dishes, buns, des-serts and whatever they want to drink. It's warm and they can dry out any wet clothes or gear they may have.

But it's a tough place to catch a little shut-eye if you need it. Some of the mushers try to sleep sitting upright in chairs at the tables, or leaning against the wall in a chair. Others prop them-selves up in the corner or drop their head on a table while around them the fans party.

Harry Sutherland fell asleep at one of the tables in 1986, then woke up to find himself surrounded by a group of Japanese tour-ists who split their attention between observing him and watching the early morning cartoons on the bar television.

"I don't think they understood either me or the TV."

Frank Turner tries catching a little shut-eye under the pool table. He gets kicked occasionally by players and a beer is dumped on him. He crawls out and beds down on top of his sled. It's cold, but it's quiet and dry.

"Really can't blame them," he says, "They are a business and it is an opportunity to make some money. They try to make it comfortable, but it's not really a place where we can totally relax. A lot of us just feed and water the dogs then keep on going."

Bob Bright couldn't sleep if he wanted to when he arrives. His stomach is tied up in knots over the condition of his sled. It has taken a beating on the trail and he isn't sure if it will survive the next stretch of trail. Titanium parts for repairs are proving to be difficult to get a hold of.

Jim Reiter arrives in a buoyant mood. Everything has gone just fine. The team is healthy and happy. So is he. And nothing has been left behind. He smiles as he watches Debbie Styer walk towards him. It is nice of her to drive up here just to see how he is doing, he thinks, but he wonders why she isn't smiling. Then he puts his hands in his pockets and feels a set of keys.

Mary Sheilds is just happy to be anywhere. Whether she's on the trail or in a checkpoint, she always seems to be happy. The only woman to complete both the Iditarod and the Yukon Quest, the amiable author of books on dog mushing and life in the northern wilderness walks down her line of dogs flashing her trademark smile. She gives an affectionate rub and talks quietly to each of "her guys."

Nineteen years ago, as a Wisconsin high school student, she came north to work for the Camp Fire Girls in Alaska and fell in love with the land. When she graduated, she returned to live out her adventure fantasy by living in the wilderness and running dogs. Even after two decades, the thrill has not jaded.

In random order over the next several hours, the mushers pull in.

Dave Monson. Kathy Swenson. Rick Atkinson.

Jim Bennett, a former teacher from Fairbanks. He took up dog mushing when he got tired of having his snow machine break down in the bush all the time. This is his second Quest as a driver; in 1984, he was the Quest's first president of the board of directors.

Tom Randall of Whitehorse pulls in. Tom is a truck driver who at one time restricted his winter excitement to operating his snow machine while his wife Elsie drove a few dogs. When she got sick, he had to run the dogs. His first night out with them he seemed to be taking a long time to come back home. So Elsie dragged herself out of bed and went looking for him. When she caught up, he was still mushing along the trail towards who knows where and loving every minute of it. He still is, six years later.

Lorrina Mitchell. Ralph Tingey. Gerald Riley. Ron Rosser. Grandmother Lena Charlie, the oldest female to ever race the Quest, arrives. At 58 years of age, having worked as a trapper and dog musher for her entire life, she feels she now has the spare time required to indulge in a leisure activity. Besides that, three of her own children and two of her grandchildren are involved in racing dogs and she doesn't want to be left out of the fun.

Not all the drivers arrive tonight. Stragglers wander in occasionally during the next morning and afternoon. The last to arrive is Mike "Rattles" Kramer.

The first 75 miles have taken their toll on his dogs. They are in no shape to tackle the next stage. After 24 hours on the trail already, Kramer himself is beat. He quits the race.

The Arctic air mass is delayed in its advance to the south. The first afternoon of the race was rather pleasant, but a brisk northern wind is now sweeping in the bone-numbing cold. Up above, the stars and moon are gradually obscured by a billowing bank of clouds. There is no fresh snow falling, but the wind, gusting up to gale force, will compensate for that by drifting a lot of the old snow.

It is the worst combination of environmental conditions at the worst possible time. Above the lodge at Angel Creek looms the silhouette of the first of the three major mountain ranges that stand between the drivers and the finish.

Footnotes

1 The Iditarod is another of the 1000-mile sled dog races. It runs from Anchorage on Alaska's south coast, through the interior to Nome, on the north coast of Norton Sound. The race takes it's name an abandoned gold mining town midway along the route.

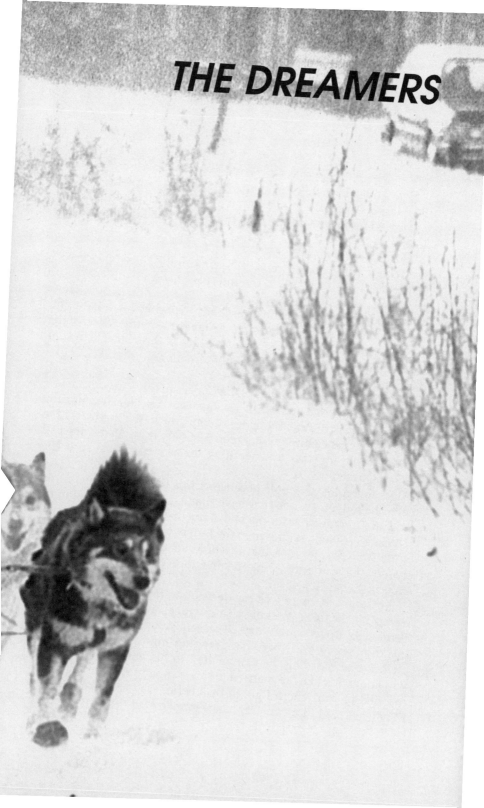

THE DREAMERS

Every once in awhile, as he sits at home playing with his cats, the question filters through his mind. "Why in hell is a Mississippi boy mixed up in something like a dog race when I don't even like dogs?"

The answer is easy.

"To me a dog sled race is still just simply a dog sled race," grins Roger Williams, "It's the international and philosophical aspect of what we're doing. Sitting down with people from Alaska and the Yukon and everybody working for a common goal. That's what keeps me going. As far as the competition of the race . . . hell, that only lasts two weeks out of the year. The rest of it. The complexities of running an international event. The logistics. The politics.

The different philosophies of the Canadians and Americans. Of the people who live in the villages versus urban life. Here in Fairbanks we think differently than say someone living in Mazie Mae or Biederman's Cabin or wherever. The only thing that brings all those people together and working for a common cause is the Yukon Quest.

I've met a lot of people because of this that I probably would never have met. People that have made a lasting impression on me that I'll remember for the rest of my life."

When Williams sat down in the Bull's Eye Saloon in the spring of 1983, he had no idea that it would change his life. But major changes have a way of happening to Williams when he least expects them.

For example, there was the decision to move to Alaska in the first place, in 1975. Working as a chemical engineer in Memphis, Tennessee, Roger found himself on call 24 hours a day. Responding to a phone call that was dragging him out of bed at two o'clock one morning, he commented to his wife Jocelyn. "Hey, you know. It's like I'm married to this company and I'm not really married to you. There's got to be a better way to make a living. Maybe we should move. Or change jobs."

"Why don't we move to Alaska?" she responded. So they did. And there was the spot where Williams began his love affair with northern history, a fascination that was to mould his role in a sport that he had, and still has, limited enthusiasm about. It was in the spring of 1981, during a stop-over in Whitehorse, Yukon. They were camping during an early winter drive up the Alaska Highway, spending every night shivering in a tent in minus 20 degree temperatures. Eventually, Jocelyn decided that being economical could take a back seat to being warm. "I want to spent the night in a hotel room," she said, "In a real bed." And Whitehorse was the next stop on the road map.

For a small city (about 20,000 inhabitants), Whitehorse is surprisingly cosmopolitan: featuring facilities that one would expect to find only in larger centers. One of those facilities is a small log building that houses the McBride Museum.

Williams is an insatiably curious man. He loves to discover things or research them. Museums are of particular interest to him. Since both Jocelyn and Roger had had a good night's sleep, he decided to spend a couple of hours browsing through the small log building. He would never look at the north in quite the same way again.

"I could live in that museum. It's just packed full of a lot of good stuff. Anyone that lives in the Yukon or Alaska should go through there because there's well-preserved newspaper articles, histories of the gold rushes in Alaska and the Yukon, a lot of colourful stuff on some of the characters back then. I think it's one of the finest museums for a town that size I've ever seen."

For two days he prowled from room to room. Here he discovered nostalgia that harkened back to a time before airplanes, highways, radios and telephones.

He uncovered the fabled mystique of the gold that lay hidden under the ice and snow for centuries. A history measured in ounces and lives lost or ruined in its pursuit. He found a time when there were true heroes: some lauded for their feats, most unrecognized since being a hero was just a way of life.

In his own way, he became like a dog driver, seeking the romantic fantasy of the pioneer. But rather than trying to find it on the back of a sled following the spirits of the long-dead mail drivers who preceded him, Williams sought to understand the common threads that joined the Yukon and Alaska through a shared history and the unique society which that legacy produced.

"We are really one distinctive type of people, those of us who live either in the Yukon and Alaska and the Northwest Territories by choice. The only thing that really divides us are political boundaries."

Possibly it was that shared fantasy that was the basis of the friendship between Williams and his co-worker at the Fairbanks Daily News Miner, Leroy Shank — a recreational dog musher. On the surface, they have little in common. Williams is slender. Shank is heavyset. Williams's education comes from universities and colleges. Shank's book-learning comes mostly from having little else to do while on his trapline except read: like most of the dog drivers who live or have lived in the bush, it is a highly developed, although unconventional education. Williams likes cats and hates dogs; Shank loves dogs and hates cats.

To this day Williams really can't explain how Shank was able to convince him to be the handler for his dog team in the 1983 Angel Creek - Bull's Eye Saloon sled dog race. But for whatever reason it was, the decision to help his friend set him up for one of those unexpected moments of great change.

There were four of them at the table in the Bull's Eye Saloon following the race: Williams, Shank, Ron Rosser and Willie Libb, a Fairbanks musher who specializes in sprints and middle distance races. The beer was flowing easily and the imaginations of the drivers started to get fairly well lubricated. It started out as a casual comment, something like "God, this is a fun race. Wouldn't it be nice if they made it a little longer?"

From there it started to get longer. It went past Angel Creek to Chena Hot Springs, over the mountains to Circle Hot Springs, to Circle. Williams was enjoying the flights of fantasy, but attached no importance to them until the race hit the Yukon River and turned southeast towards the Canadian border.

"Once we got to the Yukon River, I thought, 'well shit. We're at the Yukon River, there's a trail right there all the way into the Yukon. We could run a race, an international race and it also follows a historical trail. We could really do something that makes a statement.' "

As the bar bill got longer, so did the race. Eventually it got all the way to Los Angeles. When Williams woke up the next morning, there was a glowing ember of an idea in his head, but his hangover took precedence for the moment and the idea was left to linger on its own for the next few months.

It wasn't until he and Shank went fishing during the summer that the spark burst into flame and he found he wasn't alone. That same ember was lying smouldering in Shank's mind as well, although for entirely different reasons.

Unlike Williams, Shank's whole life has been involved with dogs. His father raced dogs in Colorado during the summer and in winter used them for hunting coyotes and for trapping. Shank was the youngest of three children, and the only boy. They lived in a lightly populated part of the mountain state and having neighbours was more an expression of longing for company than it was reality. His father's dogs were his closest friends as he grew up.

"When I was a child everyone would ask me, 'What are you going to do when you grow up?' and I'd say, 'I'm going to live somewhere where I can have lots of dogs and be a bachelor.' "

The opportunity to do both came in 1960 when his brother-in-law called him from Fairbanks. "Hey Leroy," he said, "You know you've always wanted to come to Alaska. I have a job for you."

"I'll be there in a week," he replied, and he was.

It was heaven for Shank. The 1960s were the heyday of big game hunting in Alaska. A lot of the interior was still relatively unexplored and Shank spent his summers collecting an array of hunting trophies and taking fishing trips. In the 1970s he started trapping in winter, but he chose a snow machine over dogs.

The bachelor part of his ideal lifestyle ended in 1974 when he married his wife Kathleen. The dog part started in 1977 when he decided to switch from a snowmachine on his trap line to something more dependable and less susceptible to the vagaries of the climate — a dog team.

Shank had heard about some race called the Iditarod and talked to some of the mushers who competed in the Anchorage-to-Nome classic, but he swore, "I'm never going to race." "Never say never" is a rule of life that Shank had yet to learn. Five years later, in 1982, he found himself at the start line in Anchorage and two weeks after that, he crossed under the finish line. In 1983, he did it again. But, while the idea of a long distance race still attracted him, the Iditarod itself didn't exactly thrill him.

He felt the race catered to the elite racers, the big-name competitors, and that campers like himself were treated somewhat like second class citizens.

"I said, there's got to be something besides this. I mean, there's got to be more to long distance racing or there's got to be an alternative.

Alternative. That word kept going through my mind. And I also thought of all those people in Fairbanks that invested all their time in the Iditarod. And they have to drive 500 miles just to start. And you finish in Nome. There's no highway back. You have to fly. It's expensive. And I thought there's got to be something from Fairbanks."

The conversation in the Bull's Eye Saloon just a month or so after Shank finished his second Iditarod suggested a route, one that was very viable.

It wasn't the first time a race between Fairbanks and Whitehorse had been talked about. A group of mushers, including Ron Aldrich[1], Ralph Nestor and Harry Sutherland, had become disillusioned with the Iditarod by 1976. Sitting together on Montana Creek that year, they discussed the concept of a race between the two cities. But when the group dissolved following the conversation, so did the idea.

In that summer of 1983, with their idea now burning strongly, Shank and Williams expanded their twosome to include Bud Smyth and writer Rod Perry, both veterans of organizing and racing in the early days of the Iditarod. They had to determine a basic premise. Something that would distinguish their race from any other in existence.

"We heard from Bud how, in the early Iditarods, when you broke your sled you just fixed it," says Williams, "He said, take a little baling wire along with you, a little duct tape, if your sled gets busted up, then you fix it and you keep on going[2]. We thought that was a real good idea: to make the race one where the person had to be a survivor, a carpenter, the whole nine yards."

They approached Rosser, Libb and the other mushers who had been involved in the Bull's Eye Saloon conversation. But, for them, it had been pure fantasy. Such a race wasn't feasible.

If the expertise and support to develop the idea past this point wasn't going to come from other mushers, it would have to be bought.

"We came up with a basic idea of what we wanted the race to be, then we started recruiting veterinarians, lawyers and mushers. We decided to approach this the same way my grandfather would approach an attorney.

He told me once, never walk into an attorney's office and ask him what to do because he'll philosophize you into bankruptcy. So we approached all these people and we said, this is what we want to do; you put it together and show us how to do it."

By the end of the summer, there was a definite set of rules, a specified route and even a potential starting date: February 25, 1985 — sixteen months in the future.

It was time to go public. Fairbanks Daily News Miner sports editor Bob Eley liked the idea, but didn't think it would pass the rest of the editorial staff. "I can pass it through," he said, "But those people up there aren't really wild about dog sled races."

Eley underestimated the appeal of the idea. In its first try at publicity, the race dominated the front page of Fairbanks's largest newspaper. He also underestimated the impact the race would have on his own life. Like almost everyone else touched by the race, he got involved, eventually becoming a board member and the president of Yukon Quest International in 1988.

The first public meeting didn't fare quite so well. Only seven people showed up. A second meeting drew thirty-eight people, many of them reluctantly allowing themselves to be dragged along by those who were at the first meeting. The ranks of volunteers and organizers started to swell.

It was slow but the Fairbanks end was starting to come together. But one string still left untied was the other end of the race itself. It was time for the Fairbanks organizers to contact someone in Whitehorse to develop an organization to set up that half of the proposed race. Williams, Shank, Perry and Smyth headed south in October to meet their potential Canadian counterparts, Lorrina and Gordie Mitchell and the Quest's first Canadian race manager, Wendy Waters.

It had taken Lorrina Mitchell one night and the better part of a bottle of whiskey to get Waters involved in the Yukon Quest. Waters, who had founded and organized the 220-mile long Percy De-Wolfe Race between Dawson City, Yukon, and Eagle, Alaska, in 1981, had sworn off organizing races in 1983.

The first Yukon Quest would test her skills to the limit: but in the end she would succeed in putting in 500 miles of trail and establishing checkpoints in a territory that was even more reluctant than Alaska to accept the Yukon Quest as a reality.

Race date is announced at first meeting of Alaskans and Yukoners
L-R (standing): Leroy Shank, Rob Perry, Wendy Waters
L-R (seated): Bud Smyth, Lorrina Mitchell, Gordie Mitchell, Roger Williams

Huddled in their car somewhere along the Alaska Highway, for some reason — no one seems sure exactly why — the Fairbanks group decided to take a gamble. When they arrived in Whitehorse, they announced a new starting date: February 25, 1984.

They now had only four months to put it together. It did seem a little foolhardy. At this point they had no entries, few volunteers, no checkpoints, no trails and no trailbreakers. They just had a set of rules, a lot of work to do and a lot of faith. It was a risk, but if for some reason the race didn't go as announced — like nobody entering because of the short notice, they hoped they could still save some face if they had to postpone.

In fact, both Shank and Williams almost hoped nobody would show up to enter.

The point of no return turned up in the tall, gangly body of Murray Clayton. The commercial fisherman from the coastal town of Haines stood in the back of the room at Ryan Junior High School in Fairbanks, quietly listening to the third public meeting, held in Fairbanks a week after the announcement of the starting date.

YUKON CHALLENGE

As the meeting dissolved, he pushed forward through the crowd until he reached the table at the front. Like others in the room he held out a cheque. Unlike the others, who were throwing in $100 each to help finance the venture, his cheque was for $500: the cost of entry.

"I want to be the first one to sign up and run it this year," he said. The prattle of voices around the table died away. There was silence.

Shank looked shocked for a moment. Then he reached out and took the cheque. "O.K.," he choked out the words, "It's on. This is it. We're going."

Williams felt panic well up inside himself. Hey Murray, wait, he wanted to say, Wait until we're sure we're going to do this. But he kept his mouth shut. Whether it was the best thing or the worst thing he ever did in his life is a question he'll never really find an answer for.

Williams keeping his mouth closed and Shank reaching out for Clayton's cheque that night put both of them on an emotional roller coaster that was just beginning its ride. It would disrupt their professional lives and their personal relationships with their families and friends. In some ways, seven years later, it still does, even though their involvement has been reduced significantly.

For the four months leading up to the first Yukon Quest the organizers, and a gradually increasing number of volunteers, lived for nothing else except the race. Committees were set up to oversee the multitude of details that had to be covered. An executive group was established, with positions often filled for reasons beyond belief.

In one meeting Jim Bennett stood up to make a point. He drew a circle on the blackboard to represent the financial pie that he was now going to slice into its various pieces of need. It was a good circle, almost perfectly round.

"You're president of the association," said Shank, "I can't draw a circle that good." Everyone else agreed.

The financing that Bennett started to cut up came from various and unexpected sources. One of the first was a phone call from the manager of Sampson Hardware, one of Fairbanks's oldest retail stores, "My name is Mark Webber," said the voice on the other end, "I want to give you people some money."

Shank didn't get a speeding ticket on his way to pick up the $10,000 cheque, but he should have.

Another call came from a middle-aged widow, who was scheduled to undergo serious surgery later in the week. "I read in the newspaper about your race," said Alexandria Ross, "I would like to donate $1,000." She became the first life member of Yukon Quest International, the association set up to organize and administer the race.

Not everything went smoothly. The logistics of putting together a 1000-mile race through the wilderness exacted a toll on the endurance of the organizers. The stress ground away at the most patient of the workers and even the usually amiable Bud Smyth leaped up at one meeting screaming at another volunteer, "Stand up you son of a bitch! I'm going to knock your lights out."

But Williams and Shank had laid down the ground rules. The race took top priority. Regardless of emotions, personalities or philosophical clashes, the race came first and what was good for the race was all that was important.

Distance can cause great problems in communication and trying to organize a race with the start and finish line a thousand miles apart and in two different countries was often difficult. The fact that it was mid-winter didn't help either.

Williams and Shank drove out of Fairbanks one morning, headed for a meeting in Whitehorse. It was cold when they started, about minus 50, and it just kept getting colder as they headed south. Eventually the car's fan belt froze and broke, delaying them for several hours.

They arrived in Whitehorse, too late for the meeting which had ended a couple of hours earlier. Only two of the Whitehorse group were still in the hotel where the meeting had been held - Jon Rudolph of Whitehorse and Bruce Johnson from Atlin, B.C. The two men had been sitting in the bar since the meeting had ended. Their topic of discussion had focussed on the failure of Williams and Shank to make it to Whitehorse and the problems of dealing with the Alaskans via long distance. The sight of the two overdue Americans spurred them into action.

They launched themselves at Williams and Shank, pushed them against the wall, and then, uninhibited and outspoken as only an excess of drinking can make a person, they vented their feelings.

Shank, his face sombre, looked over at Williams, "Goddamn it Roger," he said, "Try to make heroes out of these mushers and all the bastards can do is complain."

44

A trip into the Circle District, north of Fairbanks, produced another revelation. "We held a meeting in Central," remembers Shank, "And about 40 people turned up. Hell, I didn't even know that 40 people even lived there."

Bit by bit, piece by piece, the organization came together. Twenty-seven mushers entered the race. One thousand miles of trail were broken and marked. Seven checkpoints were established. Tons of dog food were shipped in. Aerial support was arranged and communication systems were set up.

By the time "Pecos" Humphries made history by starting the first Quest, even the $50,000 purse for the winners had been guaranteed (the purse consists of the entry fees from the mushers plus monies donated for that purpose).

For Williams and Shank, there was a moment at the start line when the noise of the crowd and the barking of the dogs seemed to fade away and there was a silence that only they heard. In that moment, they paused briefly to shake hands in quiet celebration.

But full realization of what they had accomplished came individually to each of the two men at different times and places along the trail.

For Shank, it came in Eagle almost a week later, when he watched the first musher, Sonny Lindner, driving his sled on the Yukon River below the spectacular rise of Eagle Bluff.

"It was in the morning and that sun was beating down there and you could see Eagle Bluff and he came around that corner through that beautiful white snow. And just as he popped around that corner, that church bell started ringing. And man! That just sent chills up my spine . . . I had tears in my eyes. I just said, 'Good grief.'

And all those people were so excited because they had never seen a race before. They didn't even care who it was. They just said, 'Oh my God. Look at that. It's happening. It's him.' "

Williams's moment had to wait a little longer. He was well ahead of the teams, making sure that checkpoints were up and operating before the teams arrived. One of them, at Dawson City, they got set up and organized just 10 minutes before the lead driver, Joe Runyan, arrived. It wasn't until Williams stood in Whitehorse, waiting at the finish line for the Yukon Quest's first champion to arrive, that he had a chance to consider all that had passed in the previous few months.

He thought back to one particular moment in that time, when the two of them, Williams and Shank, went to a meeting where all "the pillars of the community were there and we told them what we had in mind. They all stood up and laughed. They said you can't do it. There's no possible way you can ever do it.

When Sonny crossed the finish line there in Whitehorse, we had the purse money waiting for him, everything had clicked, everything was in order. I just looked at Leroy and I could see these things in my mind where all these people were basically against us and they said, 'You can't do it. Give up before you start.'

And when Sonny crossed that line . . . if nobody else ever made it across the finish line, it could be done because one guy did it. It happened to be Sonny Lindner."

Footnotes

1Ron Aldrich is the only musher to have driven in both the first Iditarod in 1973 and the first Quest in 1984. A retired United States Air Force officer turned pilot-preacher-teacher, he was introduced to mushing as part of his survival and rescue training in the late 1940s. It was near his homestead on Montana Creek, where he uses dogs to haul his wood and water, that this informal gathering took place.

2 The original Iditarod rules dictated that the musher was to be totally self-sufficient and could not receive assistance while on the trail and in the checkpoints. However, in the past few years it has become the practice for the top drivers to have a handler look after the team at most checkpoints and to be able to change sleds when the one they are using breaks or when their strategy in the race demands a different type of sled. This was part of the inequity that Shank didn't like. The smaller kennels, like himself, can't afford to have a handler in the checkpoints or to have more than one sled.

LIFE IN A
PING PONG BALL

Up here there is only Boreas: the north wind. Nothing moves without the aid or influence of the wind. It is moody, sometimes showing the harsh side of its disposition. It rears up, then crashes down, roars furiously off to the south, then turns and charges back north. It spirals, as if to burrow a hole in the earth or build a funnel to the stars.

It strips the mountain bare, exposing a dark, surrealistic landscape of weathered rock and twisted frozen vegetation, then deposits massive quantities of snow into drifts that tower into the sky.

The wind doesn't know its own strength in such rages. It tosses entire teams and sleds carelessly over cliffs or across glaciers without even expending a pittance of its power. It has substance, spitting crystals of snow that cut and sting like shards of broken glass or that settle on the skin, creating a crust of ice that pinches the eyes shut or burns into the flesh.

Or the wind can be gentle and compassionate, giving the drivers a gentle pat on the back and an encouraging push from behind.

It is best when it's at rest. The snow crystals can hang motionless in the air, a massive suspended prism through which the sunlight can create a shimmering wall of colours like a rainbow that isn't satisfied with just arching through the air, but wants to fill the whole sky.

The wind is a musician, playing for whatever audience that dares to listen. From the soft melodic hush of snow being moved over snow, it builds through a rhythmic booming of gusts to the resounding sonic whistle and howl of the gale force crescendo, or drops into motionlessness, leaving pure silence.

At such times it is like the Venus Flytrap flower: using its beauty to deceive its victims into venturing nearer, then closing the trap behind them.

The human body is not designed to resist the north wind. Moving arctic air freezes exposed skin in seconds. It drains the heat from a person in minutes. As the musher works to stay warm, he or she perspires and the moisture, freezing solid in the clothes instead of being able to evaporate, turns the body's natural heating system into a potential liability.

The mind then sends confused warnings to the body: warnings that either panic the individual into making mistakes or rob them of their incentive to continue and their sensitivity to the environment around them — that encourage them to lie down for a sleep from which they may never again awaken.

It is harder on the dogs: they literally freeze-dry. The dry cold absorbs the moisture they breathe out and sucks it out of their skin faster than the musher can replace it. Dehydration is a problem in any long distance dog sled race, but its effect is magnified by extreme cold and the wind.

"Mountain running is terrifying," says Lorrina Mitchell, "You have to know enough to camp down before you go over the mountain. Some people don't and they go up with half-tired dogs. All of a sudden you're above tree line and you have two options. You can turn around and go back below the tree line. Or you go straight across and you're not sure what you're going to be running into. It's almost always windy on the top of mountains . . . the few times it isn't, it's the nicest place in the world, but usually it's the lousiest.

You hit that wind and your dogs start turning their back on it. If you've never experienced it before, it can be very frustrating and very frightening. You're in a situation you've never had to cope with before and all of a sudden you realize that if I don't get these dogs moving, I'm going to freeze. And the dogs are going to freeze. And we're going to be in big trouble."

She speaks in 1988 from hard-earned experience. In 1984, Mitchell had never encountered the mountain before she started crossing the White Mountains via Eagle Summit. Her previous mushing experience had been on relatively level terrain, along rivers and hilly bush trails.

Just miles from the Chena Hot Springs checkpoint, she ventured into new ground, up the steep face of Boulder Creek-Rosebud Pass. Once they start to climb, there is little opportunity for teams to rest. The ascent is not very high, but it is unbroken from bottom to top. There are no ledges or level spots to rest on.

Once on top, the teams are in the sparse regions of the upper end of the tree line. The trail runs along a series of ridges, then through tundra broken only by large tussocks and the occasional spindly tree. Then it climbs again, away from whatever limited shelter was provided by the sparse vegetation, onto the exposed nakedness of Eagle Summit.

The snow is unpredictable up here. Some years it is a thick blanket; sometimes it barely exists. One year, the wind created drifts so high that some volunteers camped on top of one of them and helped the teams climb over.

Once on top in '84, Mitchell's team balked, her glasses slipped, fell, then vanished into the blowing snow. Blinded by her impaired sight and the blowing snow, Mitchell, sled and dogs crashed down over an embankment. Confused and lost, she bedded down. Around her, the wind raged, frustrated at not being able to tackle her directly. It threw a blanket of snow over her sleeping bag, dogs and sled.

Another musher, Jack Hayden of Lake Minchumina, Alaska, literally stumbled across her, buried in her sleeping bag beneath the snow.

Mitchell may have been able to stay warm and wait out the storm in her little snow cave, but Hayden didn't want to take the risk. He rousted her up, stirred up her dogs, tied a rope to her sled and led them down into a more sheltered area. Once they were out of the wind, he heated up some Tang and forced it down her throat until she stopped shivering. "She was definitely in trouble up there," he said. "She was definitely hypothermic."

Hayden continued his Quest and eventually finished eighth. Mitchell finished that race just 12 hours behind him.

Kevin Turnbough, a former church minister who moved north because of his love for driving dogs, describes crossing Eagle Summit as being "like life inside a ping pong ball. You can't see anything. You don't know where you are. It's noisy. It's cold. And you get banged around a lot."

Ralph Tingey and Dennis Kogl stand at the bottom of the climb to Boulder Creek-Rosebud Pass watching as three teams struggle towards the top. Above them they can hear the winds howling and sense the burning cold just over the upper lip of the slope.

The Arctic front has arrived as predicted.

But the winds that preceded it won't go away. Up top, out of the protection of the trees, the cold air and wind combine to push temperatures close to minus 100 degrees. Even where the two mushers stand, it is minus 25. They ponder the wisdom of pushing through without a stop.

The three drivers currently climbing — Jeff King, Jon Gleason and François Varigas — are serious contenders. If they make it through the maelstrom on top, the 1988 Yukon Quest may already be over. No one will be able to catch them.

To push now, means to camp later. The two drivers talk it over briefly. Kogl, who has driven dogs for over 20 years in just about every part of the world where dog sleds can be pulled, thinks they should stay put for the moment. Tingey, a manager from Denali National Park, agrees. They decide to wait.

"We didn't want to camp up there," says Tingey, "It's a long way and there's no point in burning the dogs now. We decided to stop for a few hours."

They aren't alone. Other teams stack up behind them, and by dawn there are 18 teams backed up at the foot of the pass. Most are feeding and watering their dogs. The early arrivals have already curled up on top of their sleds in their sleeping bags. But no one dozes for long. The storm above them roars on unabated. One by one, the three ascending mushers lead their teams over the lip and out of sight.

Their disappearance puts butterflies in the stomachs of the drivers at the bottom. The waiting gets harder. Uncertainty keeps them on edge. As the hours pass, the waiting gets to some of the teams — they start packing their sleds. The three leaders can be anywhere up there: they might be hours ahead, or camped just over the top, just out of sight.

Dave Monson wants to test his team. So far, he has sat back in the pack, but now it's time to find out what his team is made of, just how well they will respond to him under duress. He is the first one to untangle himself from the crowd and head upwards, pressing his dogs all the way. By the time he reaches the winds, he knows the dogs aren't a problem, but his clothes have the potential of becoming one.

"The dogs just charged up there and I had to run with this snowsuit on. I was sweating so bad all the zippers froze. I had to pull it off and I got it down to my waist, but it would drag on the ground behind me because I couldn't get my legs out. It was like running up a 4,000 foot hill with your pants down. It was double the work to the top." One by one, the rest of the teams follow.

It is worse on top than they expect. For all his expended energy in being the first one of the waiting teams up the slope, Monson is content to sit, just down out of the wind, and wait for the others rather than charging on ahead.

They start leap-frogging each other, taking turns breaking the wind-blown trails leading towards Eagle Summit. At this point cooperation makes more sense than competition. Ahead of the pack, the three frontrunners have all run into problems.

Gleason reaches a cabin on the Steese Highway, an all-weather highway which crosses the mountains in the shadow of the summit. He has four hurt dogs: one has dislocated an elbow, the other three appear to be suffering from some form of food poisoning. He settles down to wait. If the sickness passes, he'll continue, but the health of his dogs is paramount in his mind.

A year earlier, near this same spot, he had been forced to scratch when one of his lead dogs, Dutch, froze his foot and the other leader, Timber, decided he had had enough of the uphill and headwinds and stopped running.

"When the bottom line is drawn, the dogs come first. Position and money isn't that vital," he says.

A few miles ahead of him, Jeff King is thawing out his left hand. It froze as he tried to catch a few hours sleep back on Birch Creek, in the flat area just past the Boulder Creek-Rosebud Pass.

He is using chemical heat packs to keep his hands warm, but a mishap with a power saw during the summer damaged the nerves in his hand. When one of the packs finally cools off, he doesn't notice until it is too late. His fingers are now swollen and peeling.

"I was very naive, not thinking enough. I should have known my hand would need extra care. There's such a fine distinction between the amount of sensation I did have and the zero sensation of frostbite."

His dogs are healthy and eating well. His lead dog, Hickory, actually saves him from freezing his ears as well when his hat blows off in the wind. King anchors the team, then goes after the wayward garment. But the team breaks loose and beats him to it. When he arrives, Hickory is standing with the hat under her foot.

But the 32-year-old construction worker knows his race is over. It is a bitter conclusion for King who hadn't missed a top five finish in his previous four years. The summit has beaten him. To continue means to risk freezing his fingers again and that could result in amputation.

There's a traditional saying that things, bad or good, happen in threes. For Jeff King, scratching is only the second of the three. Cutting his hand was the first. The third will come shortly before the 1989 Quest. His home will burn to the ground, killing his top two lead dogs. But, from that moment, his luck will turn because Jeff King is due. He will win the 1989 race.

François Varigas is a transplanted Frenchman who moved to a cabin on a small creek just outside of Dawson City, Yukon, because he had fallen in love with the north reading Jack London novels as a child. He has injured two wheel dogs before reaching Angel Creek, but decides to keep on running and evaluate them on the mountain. The run along Birch Creek produces a noticeable limp in the two dogs: his lead dog, Blue, also starts to hobble. When he reaches the Steese Highway, he flags down a van, loads his team into it, ties the sled to the roof and heads to Central so he can officially withdraw.

"I just decided to stop because I didn't want the dogs to pay. They were hurt. I couldn't take them to Dawson City, let alone Whitehorse," he explains.

When they reach Central, the van windows are coated with ice and it smells like a doghouse. But, says the driver, news photographer Mike Mathers, "It wasn't too bad. One of the dogs threw up, but all in all it was O.K."

Ned Cathers looking a little frosty, 1987.

The main pack of teams, leap-frogging their way through the shifting blanket of snow and headwinds, begins to crowd into 101 Lodge, the Steese Highway service station and unofficial coffee stop that provides a brief moment's respite from the elements just before they tackle the actual summit.

Working in tandem is often a necessity for the teams up here. The storm in 1984 had progressively deteriorated until some of the slower teams were stopped cold on the leeward side of the mountain. Finally five teams lashed themselves together and, led by Daryle Adkins, drove across. The ice built up on the dogs' eyelashes and froze them shut, blinding the leaders. But they responded perfectly to the verbal commands from Adkins who guided them flawlessly across the top.

The natural reaction of a dog suddenly blinded is to turn its back on the wind and huddle down. The performance of Adkins team, in overriding their instincts and placing their trust in his word, is possibly the ultimate testimony to the bond that grows between the musher and his or her dogs. But the strain of leading the crossing took its toll. Team and musher were both exhausted and Adkins scratched from the 1984 race the next day.

It is not uncommon, once up on the summit itself, for mushers to make mistakes. The winds and snow, dehydration and exhaustion combine to make it inevitable. In 1986, crossing the mountain above 101 Lodge, Frank Turner lost sight of the trail and crashed down through the snow to the bottom of a steep incline. In the howling winds and darkness, he realized he had made a mistake. Later, when the weather calmed a bit and the stars and moon contributed some light, he couldn't see anything recognizable.

"No trail. No nothing. Just a big valley and mountains. I didn't know where I was. For me it ceased to be a race. That was a survival situation. I had lost my interest in the race. I was basically worried about getting out of there. I never gave up or anything, but I was pretty concerned."

He turned his dogs loose to dig themselves beds in the snow, then sat down behind his sled, sheltered from the wind. "I didn't want to commit myself any further cause I knew . . . I was conscious that I was making mistakes and, mentally, going down the hill like that was not the proper thing to do."

The dogs were depressed. "One thing that's really important for dogs is to have confidence in the person that's back there. Every time you make a mistake or get lost and you've got to turn back, the dogs know you've made a mistake and you've lost that little bit of confidence. When we were in that predicament, they didn't want to be there and got pretty despondent."

At dawn, he spotted Kathy Swenson cutting across the hill above him. Taking his cue from where she was heading, he rehitched his team and traversed the face of the hill to intersect the trail.

It is Ralph Tingey's turn in 1988 to sit on top of the summit for hours. He learns the hard way just how demoralizing it is for a dog to run into the wind and blowing snow. His lead dog, Pearls, just decides to stop running.

"She was pulling, then all of a sudden, she got bummed out. Her ears went down, her tail curled up underneath her and she got a real sad look on her face. Then she sat down and burrowed in. What can you do? Having a lead dog balk is every musher's nightmare." For Tingey, it is a temporary stop. After a few hours, he puts Pearls further back in the team and hooks up an older leader who does the job.

The trail down follows a long steep, straight valley. The descent is over bare rock, swept clear of snow. Over top of this are build-ups of ice and small glaciers formed by overflows[1]. What makes it particularly difficult is that the teams usually have to traverse, or sidehill, their way across the ice. If they try to cross on the uphill end of the overflow, dogs and sled skid downhill. The dogs can't get a foothold and the sled 's weight simply pulls them along. If they try crossing on the downhill end, the musher and sled usually end up wallowing in deep snow and the dogs are on the ice, trying to pull. The combination of ice and rock doesn't give the mushers anything to plant their brakes into to help control the descent. Some wrap chains around their runners to create more drag. Most simply take their chances and bank on their skills in the crazy ride down the backside of the mountains.

"We had to just kind of inch our way down the hill," says Swenson, "We couldn't just go straight down. I had my sled tipped sideways into the hill and I was standing on the side of my runner as it was tipped and holding onto the side rail."

It isn't until near the bottom that Swenson loses control. She swings to one side of the trail and collides with a batch of willows. The willows spring back, and flip the sled completely over.

"It happened so fast. You're just kind of standing there wondering how in hell did I manage to do this. I had to think — sometimes that's hard to do when your brain is frozen — but I had to think about how I was going to tip it back over. It was a major decision at the time. So I just turned it back around and we just kind of fishtailed the rest of the way down. Oh, it was nasty!"

Most drivers find their sled keeps sliding down past their lead dogs, then start tumbling end-over-end down the mountainside dragging the dogs along with it. When it stops rolling, the driver straightens it up and starts the whole process over again.

Dave Monson keeps dropping his sled and having to stop to pick it up. Rick Atkinson manages to dump his sled upside down halfway down, but neither find themselves in any major difficulty.

"It was so steep," says Jim Wardlow, a Delta Junction, Alaska, carpenter. "I just rolled like a barrel while my dogs dug in and tried to hang on."

The buck brush, willows and occasional patch of soft snow absorb some of the shock of the falls, saving most of the dogs from injury. Few are hurt on the descent.

Kate Persons, who spends her vacation from her management job at a salmon hatchery in Kotzebue, Alaska, taking long distance sled dog trips, stops at the bottom of the hill. She pulls out a knife and cuts her way into her sled bag. A container of watery dog food has broken open and drenched everything inside the bag. Then it froze solid, hermetically sealing all the contents.

The rock 'n roll effect of the downhill continues it's beat in the small set of foothills grouped along the base of the mountains.

"We followed this kind of tailing² along a creek at the bottom," says Lorrina Mitchell, "And it's all glaciered and overflowed for miles. On the glare ice, all frozen and humpy, some places you'd be going 20 miles an hour, then you'd slam into something and there's no way to stop. You got your brake down and you're still going 20 miles an hour which isn't a lot of fun." Several times she intentionally lays the sled on it's side to increase the drag and prevent collisions or just to slow down.

Then, just as suddenly as the winds, ice and rock had appeared at the top of Boulder Creek-Rosebud Pass, it ends. Almost as if someone drew a line on the map and said, "Ice, wind and rock on this side. Deep snow over here."

With little warning, the teams plunge into the waist-deep snow that blankets Crooked Creek, a small stream that, in summer, flows gently from the bottom of the mountains toward the middle of the Circle District.

Under the freshly fallen snow, there is a trail. But it isn't visible and the markers are set a mile apart: too far apart to see from one to the next.

The teams, which had spread out a little on the summit as each encountered its own problems, bunch up again.

"Jim Wardlow and John Shandelmeier are up ahead breaking trail," Mary Sheilds informs Mitchell when she arrives, "The trail's real narrow and we can't find enough markers to know where to go."

It isn't hard to identify the route when they find it. But if they step off the packed trail, the mushers sink down to their hips and the dogs up to their ears in snow.

The mushers take turns walking in pairs ahead of the teams , breaking down the snowdrifts and beating out a path with their snowshoes. But it is slow going. And the trail is bent and twisted. It takes them to a point where they can see the buildings at Central, just a few miles away, then it takes them in another direction, just to give them another tantalizing view of their destination before another corner takes it away again.

Their experiences, on top of the summit and in the lower reaches of the valleys on either side, aren't without precedence. The same trails were used in the early years of the twentieth century to move supplies, mail and passengers between Fairbanks and the Circle District gold fields. Not only dogs laboured with heavy loads over the mountains, horses also were used to pull sleds in winter.

Only with the building of the Steese Highway in 1927 was there a real road to the Circle District. However, until the mid-1980s, the Steese was a summer highway only. Even today it is subject to winter closures because of high winds and drifting snow.

What takes the mushers less than a day to cover in the Yukon Quest would often take up to a week for the larger freight sleds[3]. Part of the old trail system is now a recreational and historical trail since, other than the Quest, it is no longer in regular use.

Along its length were roadhouses, ranging in the quality of accommodation from the log cabin luxuries of Miller's Roadhouse to beds made from spruce boughs on the dirt floors of tents. Little remain of them except their reputations as hospitable places to stop.

One of the best recorded roadhouse stops was the one at Central, on the north side of the mountains. It was renowned for it's accommodation and especially for it's food then, as it is today. The mushers are heading for this small community, specifically for the motel-cafe, "Crabb's Corner", which is a Quest sign-in point.

Cafe owner Jim Crabb thinks he is ready for the teams to start arriving at Central. Usually they come sporadically. One or two arrive, sign in, feed and water their dogs, have a bite to eat themselves, then push on. Neither the cafe nor the parking area are terribly large. Three or four teams at a time is the most he can handle efficiently.

He's heard about the large group of teams at the foot of Rosebud yesterday, but that had happened before. The summit will have sorted them out. Especially with this cold and the wind that is blowing up there. That will scatter them all over the face of the mountain and they will probably be turning up in dribs and drabs all night long, he thinks.

The night starts out right. Gerald Riley and Larry "Cowboy" Smith, the taciturn Dawson City, Yukon, driver, pull in and talk with race marshal Jon Rudolph. In a while, Crabb expects a couple more teams. Relaxing over a cup of coffee, he glances out his window and gets the shock of his life.

There is what looks like a freight train rolling down the road towards him. Coming out of the darkness, there is one light after another as far as the eye can see.

"Finally," says Mitchell, "we hit another cut that heads back towards the road and we get on the road. It was a really incredible sight to see for a while cause there's all these dog teams, and we've been slogging through the snow, and as soon as they hit the road, they're loping and running-trotting fast, and they're coming down like a whole bunch of grand prix cars. All these teams, passing each other on the fly, and moving and cruising along down the road."

But the burst of adrenaline and high spirits is short. The teams are momentarily relieved at finally finding a trail they can't fall off of or have to break down with their snowshoes. But at their first opportunity, upon reaching the cafe, the dogs flop over and close their eyes.

The drivers feel lead in their arms, legs and eyelids when their sleds grind to a halt. "I'm as tired now as I usually am at the end of the race," says Rick Atkinson, "And we've barely even started. It's not a race. It's a survival exercise."

Behind them, alone in a cabin below Eagle Summit, Jon Gleason watches the silhouette of a late team drive past in the darkness with desperate envy in his eyes. His dogs just aren't bouncing back. His race is over.

Above him, the wind backs off a bit, resting for a moment and allowing the stars to peek through to the earth.

Footnotes

1 When streams are no longer able to run under the ice, they are forced to find an alternate route. The water rises to above the ice level, then leaks out and overflows onto the ice.

2 A tailing is a ridge of gravel left behind by gold dredges when they churned up the valley floor during the early and middle part of the twentieth century.

3 The old freight sleds were almost twice as long and half again as wide as the racing sleds being used today. They weighed almost twice as much, and the freight was substantially heavier than the load being carried by the mushers.

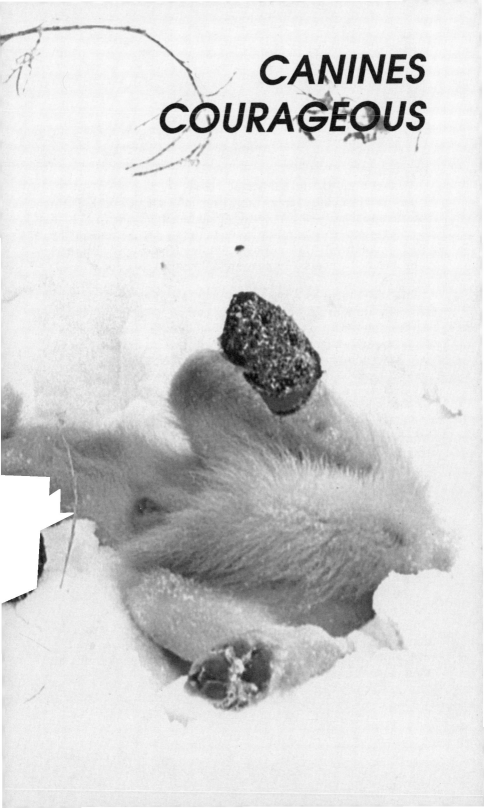

CANINES
COURAGEOUS

Draw a circle around Fairbanks, Alaska.

Inside it, include Manley (northwest), Nenana (south), Goldstream and the Chena Hot Springs road (north). Inside that circle is the greatest concentration of racing dogs on the face of the earth: more than 10,000 sprinters, middle-distance specialists and long distance runners. And they are unlike any other dog you will ever see.

The Alaskan breed, with their smiling blue-grey eyes, insatiable curiosity, upright tail with its flippant curl at the top, mottled coat of grey or brown and endearing toothful grin are distinctive. Some are downright friendly, not at all your guard dog type. If you reach down to pet them, they roll over, allowing you to scratch their belly or under their chin. Or they'll give you one good sniff, and turn their backs with a disinterested air. Some are downright surly, they'd just as soon bite you as look at you.

Shyness is the dominant trait with many of the teams run by mushers from the small isolated villages of interior Alaska and trappers like Don Glassburn. His dogs had been raised in the bush and had rarely encountered other human beings. When he paraded the team up to the start line in 1984, the dogs panicked at the sight of 15,000 people lining the street. His leaders tried to hide themselves behind the dogs to the back of them, who were making a valiant effort to crawl underneath Glassburn's sled. Glassburn spent the first few minutes of the Yukon Quest just coaxing his dogs to come out from behind him and get back in front of the sled.

The Alaskan breed bears little resemblance to the multitude of pedigrees that have combined to produce this diminutive animal. Unlike many of those purebred animals or the dogs of Jack London and Sergeant Preston, few of these racers will ever see the inside of a human home and even fewer will grow old lying at their masters feet by the roaring fire.

Sled dogs resting.

They are the heart and soul of the multi-million dollar business of sled dog racing. When fitted into a harness and hooked to a tow line, they become perfectly tuned competitive racing machines. A balanced team operates almost like the pistons in an automobile engine. As tough and conditioned as the mushers may be, the mushers rank second to the true athletes who pull their sleds.

The fact that they look like dogs is almost incidental to their true purpose for being in existence. The breeding programs that created them aren't recognized by official bodies, such as the American Kennel Club or Westminster Kennel Club, which are concerned with breed appearances. In the raising of Alaskan breed dogs, function comes before appearances. They are working dogs, not house pets or show pieces, and are bred to race.

"Pedigree isn't important," says Joe Runyan, "only performance. We're a long way from an animal that can even have a pedigree, that would be accepted as a purebred."

Runyan, winner of the 1985 Yukon Quest, the 1988 Alpirod[1] and the 1989 Iditarod, is a methodical breeder who has no qualms about adapting new ideas from other breeding programs. His

Curiosity killed a cat, not a dog. Eagle, 1984.

kennel has about 300 dogs, half of them puppies. Most of the pups won't be kept past their age of maturity: about six to fourteen months. He will sell most to other mushers for breeding and give away the others.

Only the ones that show signs of what he is looking for will remain with him. The culling process for the pups is based on the method used by breeders of homing pigeons: the bird makes it home, or it doesn't. The dog meets his standards, or it doesn't.

"Everyone has their own style. Some people like dogs that are fast and quick. Some like dogs that trot at moderate speed for long periods of time. Everyone looks for dogs with attitude." Most mushers believe that a dog is no better than the puppy it was. If a pup spooks easily, has mood changes without warning or picks on other dogs, it probably has head problems or an attitude that won't fit in with other members of the team.

Bill Cotter looks for dogs that can quickly relate to him, then watches them with a critical eye for their gait, seeking dogs that move easily and are light on their feet. He likes happy dogs, that are willing and eager to go.

He is slow at culling out the pups, usually keeping all of them until they're at least a year old. Sometimes, he has discovered, slow starters turn into good dogs.

Dave Monson has a clear picture of exactly what he's looking for. "We're dealing with a working dog, with a specific function. In our case, we're working specifically with long distance racing dogs. They have to have certain physical attributes that enhance their performance: good feet, good appetites, good trotting speed as opposed to good loping speed. They have to be hard workers and that is a function of having what we call a good head or the mental desire to perform after they're fatigued or don't particularly feel like going anymore — when they'll get up and perform out of a relationship-bonding with the musher and not every dog has that.

Many things can be taught to a dog, but they cannot be made faster than they naturally are and you can't teach heart. If a dog with all the physical attributes doesn't have heart, it will never be a good sled dog. The perfect dog is one whose feet are sound, it's extremely fast and it never wants to quit."

But perfection is rare and the bionic dog doesn't exist — yet. It has taken generations of dogs and years of careful mixing and matching to produce the current version of the Alaskan Breed and everyone is constantly searching for methods and dogs that can advance the process.

The toughness of the Alaskan Breed comes most likely from a strain called the Yukon River village dog. They weren't the best looking, but only the strong survived in the isolated environment of the small interior villages. The best were bred with the best, producing teams that dominated the early years of sled dog racing in Alaska. Teams from Huslia, Ruby and other Yukon River villages would drive four or five hundred miles just to get to the start line of a race. Tough by nature, the village dog just got stronger from their extra work and inbreeding over the years.

As the mushers got more technical and the racing more professional, breeders began introducing specific types of dogs for specific reasons.

Siberian huskies had good feet. Malamutes were a smaller dog. Larger dogs ate more food, were generally slower and more prone to injury. "A light little dog that looks like a marathon runner is more likely to go the distance than a big Sumo Wrestler dog," says Monson.

Tow Line

The Belgian sheep dog was introduced because they are more responsive to people and can establish a superior bond with a driver. Gordon Setters, easily trained and conditioned, were added. Even wolves were tried, but rarely were they bred successfully. Greyhounds were introduced for speed and long legs.

"What we look for is a longer-legged dog," adds Monson, "because in each step, the taller dog goes maybe two inches further than the shorter-legged dog. If the dog is fast, the ability to move their legs is fast. If you are travelling two inches further with each step, every hour you could be travelling a mile or so further. Over 10 or 12 days, that adds up."

Certain combinations of breeding worked better than others and as the lines were inbred further, the chances of a successful high bred dog were further enhanced. Genetic or inherited problems can be reduced as a breeding line gets older. But there were still too many unknown factors. Certain cross breeding that should have worked, didn't, for no apparent reason.

Breeders like Kathy and Rick Swenson, have turned to science to aid them in developing a superior dog. They conduct urine tests on each dog, checking protein levels. The results tell them about certain factors, such as the lactic acid level in the dog's system: low levels indicate that a dog has good muscles and is able to recover quickly from fatigue. "We won't breed a dog unless it's clear on all those tests that we have what we want."

Runyan is exploring the possibility of the Franconi Syndrome, apparently well documented in humans, being present in dogs. It is allegedly connected to the efficiency of the kidney in breaking

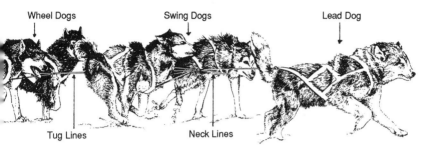

Wheel Dogs   Swing Dogs   Lead Dog

Tug Lines   Neck Lines

down amino acids. That could be a factor in performance, particularly in reducing the time required to recover after rigorous, stressful exercise. "A dog without Franconi Syndrome can bounce back faster than one with it."

Monson does a regular blood chemistry analysis of his dogs to determine fitness levels during the training and conditioning process. "It can tell you whether the dog's fighting an infection, whether the dog is anemic, whether they've been stressed too much and whether your feeding program is the right one for what you're trying to do."

Not all dogs are born equal. Some will become wheel dogs: the tandem of pullers who run closest to the sled. Their job is to redirect the nose of the sled so it follows the team smoothly as they corner or to jar the sled loose when it's frozen into the snow or ice. They take a beating as the sled will often bang into them from behind when they slow down, and they absorb most of the stress on ascents when the sled drags them back.

Even though they do most of the hardest work, they are not necessarily the biggest dogs in the team. However, they are the dogs who look over their shoulder most often to see what is happening behind them since they pay the highest price when a mistake is made.

"I like a real strong dog with fairly short legs, with a low centre of gravity. On a tall dog, the tug line is at an angle, pulling his hips constantly into the ground. A smaller dog pulls off his shoulder," says Ed Salter, "I like my big dogs right ahead of him."

Ralph Tingey booting his dogs, 1988.

Ahead of the wheel dogs are the team dogs. Once the wheel dogs have the sled moving, the team dogs role is to follow the example set by their leader and maintain the momentum. They just have to pull and be able to maintain a solid pace. But a team dog isn't always solely a team dog.

Extra wheelers are carried in this group so they can be rotated with the regular wheel dogs, giving them a break from the most physically demanding position. It is also the place to carry extra leaders for the varying conditions which are encountered on the trail. Sometimes a shrewd driver will hide an extremely fast leader as a team dog for most of the race, then put him or her up front for the final sprint.

The swing dogs are the two animals just behind the lead dogs. Their job is to keep everyone on track and let the leaders concentrate on leading. If the team starts to drift sideways or some of the team dogs try to take a short-cut around a corner, the swing dogs pull them back on line.

Strung out 40 feet in front of the driver are the lead dogs. On the slight shoulders of these animals rests the heavy load of determining success or failure for the entire team. "They're the dogs that provide the motivation for the other dogs," says Gerald Riley, " The other dogs are lost without their leaders."

Lena Charlie puts all her faith in the animals she puts up front. "They're the ones you can trust, the ones that listen. They know their way around and they're smarter than the other dogs."

Most breeders believe that leadership is an inherited genetic trait, therefore male leaders are bred to female leaders. Often the newborn pup who crawls out of the litter first or bosses around the other pups is a potential leader. Then, three or four years in harness with an old leader will give the dog the training it needs to develop their natural talents.

The leaders are developed as specialists. There are "gee-haw" or command leaders. They respond without question to verbal commands from the driver[2]. Pace leaders are fast dogs who can motivate the team to a greater speed. Storm leaders are the dogs that function well in adverse weather conditions and will head into a stiff wind without flinching. Passing leaders aren't distracted by other teams and are good at frequently passing other teams. Trail leaders can find trails which are disguised by freshly fallen or drifting snow, and can use their trail sense to find the correct trail.

Trail sense is instinctive. It can mean the difference between thin ice on a river and the safest route, between being lost or running true across miles of ice or trackless tundra. "If there is a trail, but you can't see it," says Stan Bearup, "he'll find the trail. He'll sniff it out."

Some dogs can do it all. They are rare, those dogs with the physical gifts and burning desire to perform beyond expectation. Some breeders, such as the Swensons are blessed with having bred more than one: Andy, who was up front for four Iditarod wins and Sonny Lindner's 1984 Yukon Quest win. And Mustard, who was co- lead for two Iditarod wins and spearheads Kathy Swenson's team in the 1988 Quest.

"The dog is fast, level-headed in tough and sticky situations and can run up front all day long," she says, "I can't imagine running without a good leader. It would be disastrous."

It is the musher who must relate to each of the dogs in their respective roles, who must understand them and communicate to them what has to be done. Each dog is an individual athlete and each has its own individual personality. There are dogs that other dogs don't get along with. Some are loners. Others are sociable and get along with everyone. A few are mischievous.

The well-dressed dog, 1985.

The musher, under race conditions, acts as a coach, stroking each one in his or her own particular way and making them believe that not only can they do everything they want to, but that they want to do everything they can.

The role of musher goes a great deal further than coaching at practices and game time. It is more like a parental relationship. The pup has been raised from birth by the musher. It has learned its driver's faults and strengths just as the driver has learned the dog's. For a dog who has been purchased by another musher at some point in its life, that same bonding can be achieved by the sharing of experiences and by similarities in personality.

The two learn to rely on each other — to trust each other beyond question. It is not uncommon for a musher to experience problems of one sort or another and have his team turn around or stop to find out what the problem is. Jon Rudolph once fell asleep riding on the back of his sled. When he woke up, still on the back of his sled, the team had stopped. His leaders had turned around and walked back to the sled and were sitting, watching him carefully to ensure that all was well.

Mushing lore is crammed with stories of mushers saved by teams making the right decision at the right time when the driver wasn't capable of it. And of teams saved by a musher managing to convince his dogs to keep on going when everything else around them told the dogs to stop. Daryle Adkins' team on top of Eagle Summit is a prime example of the bonding between musher and dog being powerful enough for the dogs to override their natural instincts.

The mushers make great sacrifices in their lives to meld this bond. They relinquish the company of fellow human beings for the most part and live in isolation with their dogs. Their homes, while comfortable, are usually left incomplete as funds are drained away into maintaining a kennel.

Harry Sutherland lives with his family in the top half of a two-story log cabin located in a scenic alpine valley. It is a perfect spot to train his team both in winter and summer and is far enough from his nearest neighbours that they don't hear the din of the 60 dogs he has tethered in the trees behind the house.

In 1988 the top floor, where the family lives, has uncovered log walls and plywood floors. It is heated by a wood stove and there is a park-like picnic table that serves as kitchen table. There are no interior doors, just curtains hanging over the openings in the unfinished walls. The lower level has a dirt floor which serves as a playground for the multitude of puppies that roam around the yard.

The unfinished look exists because Sutherland, a carpenter by trade, pours his money and effort into being the best professional dog driver he can be. He has had some reward in recording high finishing positions in both the Iditarod and Yukon Quest as well as winning a few shorter events[3].

Most years his winnings won't even come close to covering his expenses. Whatever sponsorship he can get and the money he earns as a carpenter go to cover the shortfall. But, like so many other drivers, he just can't bring himself to bail out of this money-losing proposition. It would be like giving up part of his own family.

Dave Monson could be a city-dwelling attorney — living in the "proper" suburb, driving a luxury automobile and wearing three-piece suits. Instead he lives in a small isolated cabin in the wilderness surrounded by about 300 dogs. He dresses in coveralls or jeans and a shirt and drives an old battered pickup over the narrow ungraded dirt road that leads to civilization.

The connection between drivers and dogs becomes so complete, a driver often can't make a decision on the trail without consulting his team. After scratching from the 1985 Quest near Carmacks, 65-year-old Glenn Craig, the oldest competitor to ever enter the Yukon Quest, said, "My dogs and I got together to talk it over. We decided we were just too tired to go any further."

Having a well-dressed team is essential — well-dressed not for looks, but to protect the most vulnerable parts of the dogs. Their fur coats provide more than enough insulation against the elements over most of their bodies, but their feet are extremely susceptible to damage. And a dog with sore or bad feet can't run. A small industry has grown up around footwear for the teams.

Dog booties are made from various materials and have several functions. They prevent snow from balling up between the dog's toes while they're running, protect them from brittle snow and sharp ice and provide an extra layer of insulation for sore or damaged paws. Not only do the rules make it mandatory that booties are carried, it simply makes sense for the driver who wants to finish the race.

Some dogs like wearing booties, but others don't. They have developed techniques for removing booties whether they're lying down, standing up or even running. The average team will wear out, cast off, bury and eat about 1,000 booties (about 80 booties per dog) during the Yukon Quest. A favorite pastime of racing fans at the start line is picking up the booties the dogs have managed to toss while just getting out of the starting chute.

"I've got some that as soon as I put them on, they take them off," smiles Lorrina Mitchell, "You're going down the line, you hear zip, zip as the velcro comes open. It's the dogs taking their booties off. I have some that eat them. I've had booties regurgitated a week later. They've obviously not gone through the digestive system: they come back up and you can identify them."

Foot care is vital to the team's success. Cold temperatures, running on a poor surface or in freshly fallen snow can cause damage to paws. A cut or chafing, blisters or cracks in the pads need to be protected. Booties are the best solution: they keep the foot warm and dry, combined with foot ointments. Super glue is often used to close cuts or cracks or to attach protective pieces of cloth to the bottoms of damaged feet on a dog skilled at removing booties.

The science of developing the racing dog's diet is a never-ending search for the perfect food. Mushers have gone from traditional diets of fish, meat and fat to commercial dry foods. The

74

manufactured food is designed to be more digestible, more nutritionally balanced and helps prevent dehydration. It also weighs less and takes up less room in the sled.

Some mushers, like Runyan, believe that a combination of the traditional meats and the commercial foods is the most efficient system. During a race the average dog will consume the equivalent of almost 30% of its own body weight each day. The meats most commonly used are highly palatable and easily digested domestic meats. The only wild game meat used is beaver, since it is the only one that doesn't carry harmful parasites. The fat portion of the diet is provided by seal fat, corn oil, chicken fat or tallow rendered from meat scraps.

Mushers don't like to change a dog's diet during the course of the race, but sometimes they have no choice. Senley Yuill, a stocky veteran of dog driving during the early days of oil exploration in the Canadian arctic, pulled into Dawson City in 1984 and ran into a distraught Pecos Humphries. His dogs weren't eating and he was getting desperate.

"What have you got?" he asked Yuill.

"Horsemeat," Yuill replied.

"I've been using chicken; I don't have horsemeat. I'll trade you a box of chicken for a box of horsemeat." They swapped and both teams thrived on the change in their diet.

It's hard to say for sure why a dog won't eat. The reasons can range from a love-sick male pining for a female in heat, to illness, to being over-stressed, to dehydration. The methods of convincing them to eat again are just as varied.

"The average person says, well, it isn't that hard to feed dogs. Well at home it isn't. They should try it on the trail," laments Jon Gleason. "You could have seven different things and the dogs won't eat the first six you give to them. But if they eat the seventh, I let them eat as much as they want of that."

Sometimes it's as simple as giving them their favorite treat. Gleason's dogs respond to chicken hot dogs; Frank Turner's are fond of regular hot dogs; Jeff King's prefer ice cream. Other times, vitamin B-12 must be administered as an appetite stimulant.

The worst reason for a dog to stop eating is dehydration. The racing animal can lose all of its body fat and half of its protein and still function. But if it loses only 20% of its water, it will die.

About 60% of the dog's weight is water. Under duress, the dog requires about a gallon of water each day to prevent dehydration. There are two ways to test for dehydration. The easiest is to pull

Snack time on the trail, 1986.

up and pinch the skin on the back of the dog's neck. When the skin is released, it should snap back down flat quickly. If it recedes slowly or remains standing the dog is in trouble. The second method is to check the colour of the dog's urine. If it is a rusty colour, the dog isn't drinking enough.

The colder or more windy it is, the more likely dehydration will occur: the super-cooled air acts like a sponge, soaking the moisture out of the dogs. Eventually they stop drinking because they've lost the desire to swallow. Tired and slightly dehydrated dogs usually won't drink water straight out of a pan. The driver has to bait the animal by making the water part of the meal. But if a dog doesn't want to drink, it won't.

"I sat down once," says Harry Sutherland, " and made beaver stew for them. So they tipped the pan over, let the liquid run out and ate the meat."

When all else fails, the only solution is rest. In his first long distance race in 1987, Ralph Tingey was startled by the effect it was having on his dogs.

"I had never seen a race-tired dog. I had never seen a dog refuse food. Refuse water. I had no idea what was happening." It took twenty-four hours of rest before he felt he could continue.

76

Sonny Lindner's team taking a break, 1984.

As the drivers get more experienced, they develop their own methods of judging when the dogs are rested enough to continue. Sutherland uses his team as an alarm clock for himself.

"I pull off the trail, feed the team, then I crawl on top of my sled for some sleep. Teams will go by us and neither I or the dogs will wake up. But when they're ready to go, they'll wake up and they'll start to yelp and bark at the other teams when they go by. That wakes me up and I know they've had enough rest, so off we go."

Personality conflicts can cause problems. If a dog gets ornery and doesn't seem to want to get along with his partner in the harness, the musher will adjust the spacing on the tug line so that dog runs alone. The other dogs will often help their teammate make an attitude adjustment by ganging up on him until the antisocial behaviour disappears.

Males trying to mount females in heat can also disrupt the rhythm of a team. Several teams have had to wait for a few hours at checkpoints or stopped along the trail when the musher fails to notice that a male has moved into a position to take advantage of the female. Once started, the act can't be stopped and the team can't run until it is completed. Two or more males jockeying for the same advantage can result in fights. The driver's only solution is to find a place in the team where the female can do her fair share of the pulling without disrupting the rest of the dogs.

Viruses, such as doggie flu, can stop a team in its tracks. They spread rapidly causing vomiting, lethargy and diarrhea. Collisions with trees or stepping into cracks can sprain wrists, dislocate shoulders or break legs. Fights can result in disabling cuts to paws, mouths, necks and legs.

Heat stress can cause dogs to lose their coordination, vomit and get diarrhea. This usually happens when a dog's natural cooling system can't keep up to the heat generated by running under a warm sun, even if the air around is sub-zero.

A musher can either try to nurse an infirm dog back to health with antibiotics or haul it on the sled, rather than making it run. Injured or sick dogs are usually dropped at the next checkpoint. Since a maximum of only four dogs can be dropped from each team during the Quest, it's in the musher's best interests to ensure the dogs are capable of completing the distance before they even start. Dropped dogs are shipped out and kenneled in the city where the race ends, to await the arrival of the rest of their team.

Some dogs do die. Gastric torsion, or a twisted stomach, can kill them. Burst blood vessels in their brains claim others. Dehydration is often the catalyst that precipitates a fatal health condition. But the mortality rate of race dogs is no higher than it is for the dog who lives a sedentary lifestyle.

Because of the bond that exists between driver and dog, the death of a team member can seriously affect the musher. Nick Erickson spent several hours alone on the ice of the Yukon River in 1984, hugging one of his dogs that had just died. Kevin Turnbough came across him, started a fire to warm him up, fed him and was able to convince him to continue mushing. Both mushers finished the race.

Lorrina Mitchell scratched in 1987 when she was psychologically demoralized by the loss of a dog. Don Donaldson does the same in 1988 as will Tom Randall in 1989.

"When you get right down to it," says Mitchell, "The care of the animal and the individual's welfare transcends all the other bullshit."

"Our dogs are beautiful animals," said Joe Runyan in his banquet address to the mushers in 1986, "They are to mushers what horses are to the Arabians and the Plains Indians. The winning or losing does not matter . . . we want to preserve the integrity of the animals throughout this race."

Footnotes

1 The Alpirod is the European entry in the world of long distance sled dog races. First held in 1988, it is a 1000-mile race through Italy, Austria, Germany and France usually run in early February. Joe Runyan is the only musher to have won all three of the world's long distance races.

2 There are four basic commands: "Gee" — go left; "Has" — go right; "Whoa" — stop; and "Hike" or "Mush" — go. The word "mush" is from the French "Marche", which means "go". It was the use of this word that gave the dog drivers the name "mushers". Most drivers also have their own personal commands for the dogs. It's surprising how they react to requests such as "Get back on the Goddamned trail!"

3 Sutherland has finished second and third in two Yukon Quests, and he has a third place finish in one Iditarod.

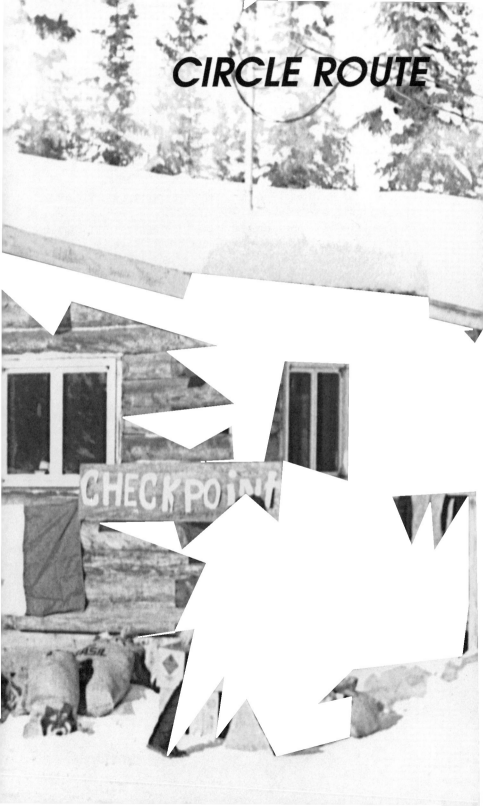

CIRCLE ROUTE

CHECKPOINT

Central is not an official Yukon Quest checkpoint . . . yet. But it has gained honorary status as an official sign-in stop — the result of the residents' determination to make their small community something special for the drivers. Their efforts have paid off. There are few sights along the trail that are as welcome for both musher and dogs as the Crabb's Corner caf, especially after a day and night spent bucking the wind on Eagle Summit and burrowing through the snow along Crooked Creek.

There's plenty of room for the dogs to curl up and get a snooze. Plenty of water, heated for food or cool for drinking. When the mushers finish tending their teams, they wander inside for a hot meal, a cold beer and a place to sleep. Since it's also a motel, there are rooms here with beds, but not everyone stays awake long enough to get to them.

Lorrina Mitchell needs some sleep. Suffering from exhaustion and mild hypothermia, she knows that, if she continues the way she is, she will become her own worst enemy further down the trail.

"But I was so hyper I couldn't sleep. I asked Jim [Crabb] for a hot buttered rum with a double shot of rum. I don't drink alcohol on the trail, but I thought I've got to mellow out and get some rest. About the time that thing hit bottom, I fell asleep in the hallway beside the bathroom. Nobody wanted to sleep there. It was too noisy. Too busy. People walking back and forth. But it was a big wide hallway, so I just curled up against the wall and never heard a thing."

Food and drinks are on the house for the drivers, and that's a rule strictly enforced.

Jon Rudolph remembers an argument he got into during his second Quest in 1986 when he decided to stay at Crabb's for an extra day. He wandered into the bar and sat down to buy himself a beer. "You're a musher," said the bartender when Rudolph put his money on the bar, "You don't buy nothing here." Rudolph explained he was only staying because he really didn't feel like leaving, not because he had to. So he wanted to pay for his beer.

"I don't care if you're staying a week," responded the bartender, "You're not buying anything here." Rudolph is back in Central this year, but as race marshal rather than a competitor. He will return as race marshal again in 1989 and 1990.

The community was originally a roadhouse called Windy Jim's on the Circle-Fairbanks trail in the early 1900s . One of the better and bigger lodges on the trail, it offered meals and rooms for travellers and miners along with stable facilities for horses and kennels for dog teams. It was a hub for trails to the various regions of the Circle gold mining district and eventually became known as Central House. When the Steese Highway, the "Road to the Midnight Sun," was completed in 1928, it went right past the front doorstep of the lodge.

The highway brought with it a change in the focus of the district. Circle City, 80 miles to the north, had been the district's main supply depot until that time because of its proximity to barge traffic on the Yukon River. But the road provided a connection via Fairbanks with the Alaska Railway and the south coast. Central profited greatly from its location on the highway and now boasts a school, a highway maintenance camp, a post office and various service facilities for the local miners, woodcutters and trappers as well as tourists and travellers.

Wilson Sam having a good time, 1984.

The hospitality extends far beyond the walls of Crabb's Corner. In 1984, when Wilson Sam, the big, amiable Native trapper from Huslia[1], lost his bag of dog booties in the storm on top of Eagle Summit, two women in Central heard the news and went to work. They, and Sam, knew the rules. Mushers had to carry a minimum number of booties for their dogs.

Jill Ruzniak and Connie Catt fired up their sewing machines and by the time Sam arrived, they had produced 85 booties for him and he was able to continue. His lost booties were found on the mountain and later turned in at Central by another musher.

After the ferocity of the weather on Eagle Summit, the trail through the Circle District is almost like a holiday for the drivers. From Central, they follow the road for about 15 miles to Circle Hot Springs. Then they swing north, heading for about 40 miles along the narrow, twisting of Birch Creek, then overland for another 40 miles on old mining and mail route roads to Circle City and the Yukon River.

"It's definitely much more restful than what you encounter on either side," says Mitchell, "It's an easy piece of trail. It's pleasant and you can just motor along and not have to worry too much."

One by one, the mushers hit the road, to cover the short distance to Circle Hot Springs. Bob Bright heads out, but there is much speculation on whether or not he will run for much longer. His titanium sled has been badly battered on the descent from Eagle Summit and the runners on the bottom have an unnatural clatter to them as he moves along the road. He searches in Central, but is unable to find anything to repair the damage with. He will try again at the Hot Springs.

Bright's high technology sleds are a source of constant curiosity among the mushers, who are generally sceptical about anything new and untried. They stick to the proven commodities, like the traditional basket sled. The basket sled works well on hard packed trails, but tends to bog down in deep snow and isn't really practical for long distance races. The drivers stayed with them until Alaskan sled designer Tim White finally perfected his toboggan sled in the early 1980s and Rick Swenson proved it was a superior distance sled by driving it to victory in the Iditarod.

The major advantage of the toboggan sled is that it's easier to repair than the basket sled. This is vital on the Yukon Quest since the rules dictate that the musher finish with the same sled they started with. White's toboggan sled has been improved on over the years and most of the drivers now use the basket sled solely for sprint, or short distance, racing.

The heavier construction of the toboggan sled is also an advantage in the long distance mushing game. "You've got to build in such durability on the Quest," says Ed Salter, a sled builder for 12 years, "For two reasons. One, you can't change sleds. And two is the fact that you carry such heavy loads."

The sleds are built using Alaskan birch, white ash, hickory, oak or maple for the wooden parts, such as the stanchions, driving bows, runners or bush-bows. The bed of the sled is constructed of high density plastics which can be cut three-quarters of the way through its thickness without breaking. But it's not perfect, as Harry Sutherland will find out in 1989 when he knocks a hole in the bottom of his sled the size of a basketball.

The same plastic is on the bottom of the runners. It protects the runners from being damaged by the trail surface. On a snow surface, a set of runner bottoms can last two to three hundred miles. But mix in a little gravel and most drivers will be changing the plastic every 30 miles or so.

DRIVING BOW
TOP RAIL

UPPER
CROSSBAR

BRAKE

BRUSH BOW

FALSE
RUNNER

RUNNER

BRIDGE

BENCHES (crossbars)

STANCHIONS

Basket Sled

The colour coding of the plastic tells the musher which plastic should be used in the different conditions. Orange is best for warm weather. Black is better for cold. White is a compromise that's durable in both warm and cold, but isn't as good in either as the suggested coloured plastic.

There was a short-lived experiment using lightweight aircraft alloys instead of wood and plastic. The alloy was very strong and the mushers liked the lightness of the sled. But when damage did occur, it was difficult to repair on the trail. So far, the mushers prefer to stick to wood and plastic sleds.

Repairs on the trail are make-shift and depend on ingenuity. In '87, Karin Schmidt used a hockey stick splint to repair a broken stanchion. She used surgical tape to hold the splint in place. Ty Duggar used radiator hose clamps to repair one of his runners, along with a combination of glue and tape.

The ultimate repair kit for any dog sled is bailing wire and duct tape. Combining those two items with a few extra bolts, some extra strips of runner plastic and a small hand drill, the musher can make repairs right on the trail. Sometimes the repaired piece is better than the piece that broke.

"I broke one runner which Shari (his wife) fixed in Dawson City," says Ralph Tingey, " She reinforced it with another piece of plastic sandwiched in and lots of bolts and we're still running that sled just that way. Her repair job was probably stronger than the original."

Toboggan Sled

Just 15 miles down the road from Central, Circle Hot Springs has long been a lure for those who enjoy the healing warmth of the geothermal waters. Bill Cotter made a point of going for a swim in the pool in 1984 after battling his way across Eagle Summit: "It felt pretty good after the night before."

Kathy Swenson found it tough to leave once she arrived in '86. She spent 16 hours, having a jacuzzi, a shower and a sleep. When she woke up, her husband Rick had only two questions, "What the hell are you doing?" and "Are you on a camping trip or in a race?"

Since the first day that gold was mined in the Circle District in the early 1900s, the local residents and visitors have used the springs to soak their tired arms, legs and backs. Almost all the mines in the area were underground. In the early days, the air in the small, cramped mining shafts below ground was choked with fumes from the coal oil lamps used for light. Above ground they fought clouds of mosquitoes in summer and sub-zero temperatures in winter. The hot water not only took the ache out of the miners' bones and the itch out of their bug bites, it also heated the cabins they stayed in while at the springs. It was almost unbearable luxury, being able to sit inside a warm cabin without having to cut wood for a fire.

The local Indians had known about the mineral springs long before they were discovered by prospector Billy Greets in 1897 and homesteaded by Frank Leach in the early 1900s. It was Leach who saw the commercial potential of the springs and built a hotel there

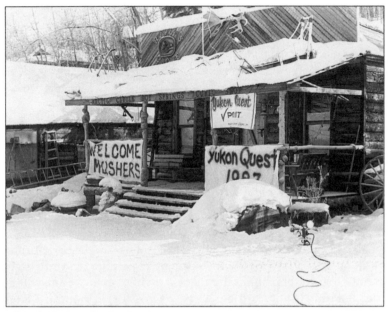

Circle Hot Springs check point, 1987.

in the 1930s. He also envisioned that aviation would play a major role in the development of the Alaskan interior and, in 1924, built the first airstrip north of Anchorage.

What Leach probably never foresaw was the existence of The Yukon Quest Air Corps. It is from an airstrip very close to that original site that the planes used for the Yukon Quest do a lot of their flying. In the first couple of years, the Quest had to rely solely on the generosity of a few small regional airlines to supply aircraft and the donation of time and planes by private fliers.

In 1987, the United States Air Force started to take an interest in the event. Part of their training is low-level aerial reconnaissance and spotting mushers for the Yukon Quest was a perfect exercise for them. While individual volunteer pilots are still a big part of the Quest, assistance from civil air patrols and flying clubs are making the job of spotting a little easier.

The business of spotting mushers from the air isn't as easy as it sounds. Identifying the individuals is important to help the race officials understand what is happening out on the trail and whether anyone is in need of assistance. The aircraft generally fly about 500 feet above the ground, tipping left, then right and banking around the corners in the trail on the ground. The passengers

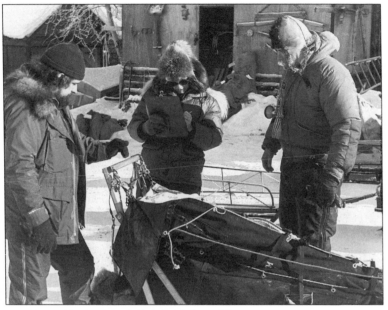

Jon Gleason (R) checks in at Circle Hot Springs, 1987.

are glued to every window, seeking out spots where teams could be stopped or watching the track where they should be running.

When a musher is spotted, it's not always possible to identify who it is on the first pass. Often a second pass is required and occasionally a third if there's something that may indicate a problem. The excitement of spotting mushers is contagious and it's hard for someone to ignore it if they're in the aircraft with the officials.

Roger Williams, Jocelyn Williams and race marshal Carl Huntington were flying with pilot Les Bradley during the first Quest, looking for mushers on the trail out of Dawson.

"Jocelyn has the best eyes of anybody in the world," said Roger, "and all of a sudden she sees a musher. Everybody, including Les, leans over and we're looking at this musher, trying to figure out who it is and I kind of look up, and there's this big hill coming at us. I reach out and tap Carl cause Les is really into this spotting. And Carl looks, and he grabs Les and says, 'Let us do the looking. You do the flying.' "

On the ground, the mushers drive comfortably, knowing that someone is up there looking over them, however the planes can also be a source of irritation.

Lorrina Mitchell, once again answering the call of nature in 1988, steps off the trail for a minute when a plane flies overhead. Then it turns back and passes over again. While the view from the sides is blocked by the bush, the view from the top isn't. A routine double-check for the spotters turns into an agonizing eternity for Mitchell. "Five minutes is a long time when you're waiting for an airplane to go away so you can look after your personal problems."

In 1987, spotters saw the tall red-headed dentist from Fort Yukon, Ron Rosser, jumping up and down behind his sled. They turned back for another look — he was still jumping. And he was still going up and down on the third fly-past. But since they couldn't see anything specifically wrong, the plane flew to the next checkpoint. A few hours later Rosser pulled in.

"What the hell were you doing out there?" asked Williams.

"The first time you guys passed," he replied, "I pulled down my pants and mooned you. Then I couldn't get my pants back up. My suspenders got tangled and I was trying to get them unsnagged."

"But those guys (the pilots) should be decorated," says Williams, "They don't have to be out there. They don't get paid. They risk their lives, just like the mushers risk theirs. And they do it just because they enjoy it."

For the moment, there are few planes patrolling the trail. The race has come to a temporary halt at Circle Hot Springs.

The resort hotel looks and feels like a carnival is about to start. Festooned in brightly coloured dog harnesses and clothing hung out to dry, the rooms populated by a crowd of freshly showered, slightly sleeping mushers, there is an air of excitement and expectation.

They wait for the ringing of the telephone — ironically one of the things the drivers live in the bush to avoid.

Somewhere ahead of the drivers, two trailbreakers on snow machines are making one more pass over the trail to Circle City. The storm on Eagle Summit last night hadn't ignored the Circle District: a layer of freshly fallen and wind-blown snow covers the area. The trail breakers are knocking down the drifts and resetting the markers along the route.

When they get to the other end, they will call. Every time a fork or knife is dropped on the floor in the restaurant, ears perk and backs straighten up. Even the deepest sleeper becomes instantly alert. Then, realizing it's not the phone, they settle down again.

90

Senley Yuill and trailbreaker near Whitehorse, 1984.

The game of "hurry up and wait" is on. The only questions are, how long will it last and who will be the first to go?

The two trailbreakers are the final link for the dedicated volunteers whose job it is to ensure that there's a safe and dependable trail through 1000 miles of wilderness. For the past two months, over a hundred men, women and machines from every community along the route have spent their weekends beating a path through the bush.

They must evaluate each section of the trail and mark it appropriately. Straight trails are marked with single markers. Corners are indicated by two markers close together on the side to which the team must turn. Once around the corner, the teams pass through a set of markers, one on each side of the trail, that tells them they've made the correct turn. Two markers forming an 'X' warns of potential danger. At places like Eagle Summit, tripods are built to tower above the snow drifts and guide the drivers in white-out conditions. Trail markers are usually narrow slats of wood, about four feet tall, with reflective circular discs on the tops.

Over 6000 markers are used each year and accurate maps are kept so the mushers can be briefed on the trail and trail conditions at each checkpoint. On the Alaskan side, the markers are mass-produced by the inmates at the Fairbanks Correctional Center. On the Yukon side, the inmates at the Whitehorse Correctional Center do their part.

The path through the bush is created using axe, swede saw, chainsaw and fires. The trailbreakers' accommodation consists of wall tents and trappers cabins. The days are long, cold and lonely. The snow is packed under the treads of snow machines; when the snow is too deep for their snow machines, they use snow shoes.

Once open, a trail usually doesn't stay open. Snowfalls and winds can close it back in almost as fast as the trail breakers open it. So, once they've opened it, they often have to turn around and go over it again, all the time battling the same elements and dangerous terrain the mushers will face when they come. Yet, like the mushers, they keep returning to do it again, year after year.

Breaking trail, like mushing, can become an obsession with some people. Last year five Whitehorse businessmen took some holidays and, rather than fly south to sunshine, palm trees and sandy beaches like most Northerners do in winter, had their own Yukon Quest. Starting a day ahead of the mushers, they drove their snow machines from Whitehorse to Fairbanks just to make sure that everything was in order along the way. They had already been on their snow machines breaking the trail from Whitehorse to Carmacks for two months prior to the trip.

The phone finally rings.

"She's open now," comes the word from the two ice-covered and exhausted trailbreakers in Circle City.

David Sawatzky, who got started in dog mushing when he bought a dog for his son five years ago, is the first one to take the plunge. An hour later, Vern Halter takes the bait. Then the exodus starts.

"The exit was incredible," says Jack Niggemyer, "It looked like a second, mass start to the race."

In the middle of the pack is David Monson, who had been the first to arrive at the hot springs. "There's no point in wasting the dogs by jumping out in front of everyone else on bad trails," he casually comments to curious reporters, "I might as well wait until others go over them and the trails harden up a little."

Behind the main pack that heads out, linger the "campers": mushers who are in the race for the experience and adventure, who entertain no fantasies of coming from behind to win in the end. Their moment of personal triumph will come when they cross the finish line, no matter how far behind the leaders they may be.

A few teams pull in as the last of the main pack trundle off down the trail. One team is bedded down at Central and still a couple more are plugging their way over a now passive Eagle Summit.

One who had arrived with the leaders, but will travel no further is Steve Mullen. "I can't hang onto my sled," he says quietly. His screw driver had slipped while he was fixing his sled and plunged through the palm of his hand. "It's a bummer," he says, contemplating his bandaged hand, "My dogs were just starting to do good."

In 1986, Connie Frerichs dumped her sled and twisted her knee as she tried to negotiate a sharp turn just a few yards from the checkpoint. She was packed to the hotel in a stretcher while her team was parked for the last time that year by her handlers. The seven-year veteran of driving dogs was back to complete her second successful Quest in 1987.

She will return again with her daughter, Terri, in 1990 as the first-ever mother-daughter pair to run the race. Both will finish as part of the "significant seven": a group of mushers who will be so far behind the leaders they decide to hold their own race within the race.

Just 80 miles away is Circle City, home of the Perry Davis's Pain Killer thermometer. This environmental device consists of four bottles set outside a window during winter. Looking out the window, a person can see just how cold it is outside. If the first bottle, containing mercury, freezes, it isn't too bad. If the second, whiskey, freezes, it isn't great, but it is bearable. The third bottle holds kerosene. If that hardens, one should hesitate before heading out. But if the fourth bottle, containing Perry Davis's Pain Killer, becomes solidified, throw another log on the fire and stay home.

It isn't frozen Pain Killer cold this year, but it was in 1987. Jon Rudolph and Harry Sutherland travelled together through this area that year. The temperatures hovered around minus 50 and a constant north wind hammered at them. "Geez, it was cold. We had to stop about every hour and light a fire, we were so bloody cold. We'd stay there for an hour, then get going again. It was bloody miserable," remembers Rudolph.

The race slowed to a crawl from fire to fire as the drivers and dogs battled dehydration and frozen feet. At one point Jeff King turned to Ed Salter whose team was trudging along behind him. "Have you ever seen a dog team go four miles an hour before?" asked King. Salter shook his head. Then it got even slower for him as his leaders started to balk against the cold. Eventually Salter's team stopped altogether and he had to turn back to the previous checkpoint for a longer rest to get them back on their feet.

Kathy Swenson remembers stopping to build a small fire for herself on Birch Creek last year. It was so cold, the ice under the fire wouldn't melt even with the heat from the flame. She soon found herself sharing it with Bill Cotter, King and Monson, who just couldn't go past a fire without stopping.

The fire is the musher's second-best friend (after the dogs). Techniques for building one range from neatly piling the wood and striking a match to dumping kerosene on a pile of drift- wood on the riverbank. Bill Cotter's bonfire building has become legendary.

"My philosophy is that if you're carrying a lot of gear and food, you're better off building fires than carrying a stove."

Cotter doesn't waste time building small fires. He drags out entire trees and piles them on the flames. They serve two purposes for him. They heat his dog food for him and they substitute for his sleeping bag. He rarely uses a sleeping bag to keep warm even when it is 60 below.

"I don't like using sleeping bags. I would just wrap a blanket around myself and fall asleep in front of the fire." That way, he reasons, when he wakes up, he will already be cold. He won't have to crawl out of a warm sleeping bag into cold air. He can warm himself up again by dragging out more trees and rebuilding the fire.

Cotter is one of the few drivers left who uses a fire to heat his food. Most of the drivers now use alcohol stoves (small round containers using a fiberglass wick soaked in alcohol) or camp stoves (which use white naphtha gas). The step from using an open fire to cook to using a stove has reduced the time required to feed a team from about two hours to under 40 minutes.

In 1990, Jeff King will find himself on the verge of a tongue - in-cheek breakthrough in improving the camp stove for the racing musher. He will have a head lamp[2] developed with a light bulb that is so hot it will keep melting the lamp lens. He will suggest

94

Camp stove getting fired up, 1986.

marketing it as a combination camp stove - head lamp.

Headlamps are essential tonight. A cloud cover hangs over the Circle District and driving in the trees makes it seem even darker. The dogs find the newly broken track with ease and the drivers sit back on their small fold-out chairs attached to the rear end of the sled. While they can watch the dogs illuminated by their lamps and dodge any overhanging branches that threaten to sweep them off the sled, their vision doesn't go any further. The light is devoured by the night.

Speed and distance become impossible to judge since there are no visible landmarks by which they can judge their progress. They know approximately how long it will take to reach Circle City, so they estimate their trip and schedule stops according to their watches.

At the end of the eighty miles of trail from Circle Hot Springs is the sparsely populated Circle City. Established in 1893, Circle City — the first major gold camp in interior Alaska — got its name when its founders erroneously believed it to be on the Arctic Circle. By 1896, boasted of being the world's largest log cabin city. It had an opera house; a hospital; a library; countless saloons, hotels and gambling halls; stores and trading posts; a U.S. Customs station and the first official post office north of Juneau. It even had it's own newspaper in 1898.

But time hasn't been kind to Circle City. The gold started to run out after only a few years and the gold seekers left soon after. The Steese Highway arrived and, instead of bringing people into the dying community, it served as an easy road out. The bustling metropolis became a shell of it's former self. Now there's only one store, one restaurant, a small post office and a school to service the 70 or so residents who are left. Not even the original historical site of this har.J-hewn log community remains, having been swept away by the Yukon River.

While they're few in number, the residents turn out in force to make sure they provide the best service possible. The effort they put in is phenomenal. There is a constant flow of hot food for everyone, and there is always someone on hand to officially greet the mushers when they arrive and to check them in.

House wife and mother Mary Dopler is one of the checkers. Her dedication to the Quest results in her working non-stop for 48 hours at a time — without sleep — until she's forced to take a break because her eyes are too glazed to see and her hands shake too much to hold anything. But the breaks are just brief enough for her to get a second wind and start over again. For a week, she will greet mushers with her ever-present smile.

"It's like a job," she smiles, "You shouldn't do it if you don't enjoy it."

It is the 200 or so people like Dopler along the trail that cause Leroy Shank to shake his head in disbelief.

"You couldn't pay people to work like that," he says, "Nobody working for wages would work that hard."

The community hall has been the checkpoint since the first Quest. It has been and still is home to the handlers, media, officials, the curious and the teams for the time they will spend in Circle. It should feel good, like an old often-used shoe, but it doesn't. Not knowing what is happening out there, but knowing what could be going wrong, keeps everyone on edge.

"At night you start thinking about all the worst things that can possibly happen. You've got to try and rationalize by remembering there are 30 to 40 other teams out there, not just one. And they'll all help each other if there's any problem," says Gordie Mitchell.

Shari Tingey, who is handling for her husband Ralph, is particularly irked by the lack of news while the teams are actually on the trail, between areas where they can be spotted. She accepts that there are times where no news is possible, but when it is and it doesn't arrive, it irritates her.

"I think as an observer, one of the interesting differences is having been at both ends of the pack. This time Ralph is close to the front, but the first year, he was two and a half days behind. And there's no one there. Nobody knows where those guys are, and I've seen it in the faces of the people, all the handlers whose mushers are way back in the pack. They have no idea where those guys are and they are just as concerned as the handlers for the people who are up front.

There's all the interest on the front of the pack, and I can understand that. But they don't keep real good track of the back. They never knew where Ralph was that first year. They had him off by days. They had him all sorts of strange places that he never was. I never knew when he was going to show up."

There is a false sense of confidence and security in the community hall as the handlers and families pick at food, talk about everything but dogs or talk dogs to the exclusion of all else.

The daylight fades and night settles in outside the hall. Then, finally, Sawatzky appears out of the dark. The checkers go out to greet him, and the nerves of the waiting handlers, whose mushers are still out there somewhere, wind up even tighter. Their eyes keep seeking the spot in the darkness where headlamps should appear. Occasionally someone wanders up the road, trying to see deeper into the night. At last, more headlamps appear, followed quietly by dogs, sleds and mushers.

Yet, while the waiting is hard, arrival more often results not in relief, but in frustration. Only in Dawson City can the handlers or family actually assist the musher. Here in Circle City, they can only watch, supply information and advice, and hope for the best.

"It's a real thin thread on the emotions out there," says Shari Tingey, "It's just a real thin thread because they are so tired. You can offer all sorts of advice, but they've got to be in the right mental state to pick up on it. The longer someone has raced and the better the racer they are, the more they'll pick up on you. You see them mentally fall off. You say something right to them, you see them mentally build up again. You say something wrong, they fall off again. You watch them go out the window and there's just no coming back."

But John Shandelmeier suggests that just the fact that there's some support for you outside of your immediate family of dogs helps, "Even if all they can do is look at you, it helps."

Ned Cathers draws up, nursing a few minor bruises on his shins. He ran through some knee-deep overflow earlier in the day, then stopped to build a fire and dry out. To speed the process, he banged the dull end of his axe head against his legs to knock the ice off.

Canadian musher Adolphus Capot-Blanc just nips American driver Cliff Cadzow at the final corner to edge into the checkpoint ahead of him. "We race at times," smiles Cadzow, "We even raced to see who would get into bed first last night. Adolphus won that too."

Bob Bright clatters into the checkpoint and announces his decision to quit the race. His sled runner is cracked and the plastic runner-bottom just won't stay attached. "The sled can't be fixed. I tried to find some parts, but they're not available."

Failure with this sled doesn't dampen his enthusiasm for the race or for trying to improve new technology for long distance racing. Next year he will turn up with a new sled: a torpedo-shaped device with an innovative brush-bow, built out of kevlar. That sled also will not complete the Quest.

Circle City is the last place that the handlers and families will have a chance to see the mushers before reaching Dawson City, 280 miles further down the trail — another reason why the handlers and families don't really feel comfortable here. The checkpoint at Eagle, about half-way to Dawson, is accessible only by airplane, dog sled or snow machine in winter.

The drivers' time here isn't spent idly. With the first long totally isolated stretch of the trail facing them, they check and double-check to ensure that everything is in order. They drag sleds into the community hall to repair them. The walls are hung with drying dog gear and clothes. Dog food is cooking in a dozen different pots where the teams lay in an open field across the road from the community hall. Mushers are sprawled across beds in the back room, sitting on bundles of hay or spread-eagled on the floor trying to get a little sleep.

The volunteers treat the mushers to the last luxury they will see for awhile. Their food is heated for them on small stoves and if it gets cold while they're eating, they can always zap it in the micro-wave. In 1984, held up by strong winds, Kevin Turnbough summed up the mushers' feelings about this checkpoint, "If I have to be stuck somewhere. It may as well be somewhere with a microwave."

Just down the road and over the bank through a patch of willows, shrouded in mist and drifting snow, the Yukon River awaits them with cold anticipation.

Footnotes

1 Wilson Sam had a completely individual approach to long distance sled dog racing. He ran the 1984 Yukon Quest almost as a public relations exercise. He spent as much time stopping to socialize with spectators and posing for photographs as he did actually mushing. His entire philosophy was summed up when he arrived in Chena Hot Springs. Jumping off his sled, he enveloped Roger Williams in a huge bear hug and loudly declared, "Goddamn, I'm having a good time!"

2 Headlamps are small, but extremely powerful flashlights that can be worn on the head by the mushers. They are powered by a battery pack, usually worn under the coat. Their purpose is to provide the musher with light while they are travelling in the

CANYONS OF ICE

The Yukon River meanders for almost 2,000 miles through the center of Alaska, bordered on both banks by pre-Cambrian mountains that predate life on earth. In some places the river runs deep, fast and narrow. In other areas the valley spreads out for miles and the river seems to be able to fill most of the basin.

She is the source of water. Rain clouds build over top of her, but few dare to unload their burden within her realm. Rainfall in the Yukon River watershed, which covers almost a third of Alaska and more than two thirds of the Yukon, is sparse. Even during the prehistoric ice ages, low precipitation along her length kept it ice free while glaciers swallowed the rest of the northern hemisphere.

In the summer, dry means warm. In winter, it means cold. While the summers are the hottest of most northern regions and often rank as summertime hot spots for North America, it is in the Yukon River basin that the coldest temperatures of the 1989 Alaska Aurora High will be reported — including the lowest temperature ever recorded in North America.

Communities along the river normally spend at least four months of each year in sub-zero temperatures. The long duration of the winter numbs a person to the environment. After a couple of months, 40 below is like 30 below — only colder. Just as man shelters himself in houses during the winter and dogs grow extra quantities of fur, the land protects itself from the cold as well. The mountains are insulated under a blanket of snow; the river shields itself with a shell of ice.

If the river would freeze in one level, unbroken sheet of ice, like a skating rink, it would be a simple matter to run the dog teams. But the face of the Yukon is not so predictable. Ice comes in its own collection of wrinkles, scars and character lines.

It can be glare ice. Flat and featureless, where distance is deceptive and the surface is too sheer for dogs to grip and pull effectively and where there is nothing to stop a sled from weaving uncontrollably from side to side.

YUKON CHALLENGE

It can be pack ice. As the river freezes, cakes of ice are carried by the current until they snag on a sandbar, a log jam or a solid band of ice, then they refreeze in jumbled heaps. Some of the pieces are as big as small cabins; others are slender, razor-edged blades of ice that stick straight up like knives.

Overflow ice — water from streams running into the river — forms a jagged fan shape when frozen or a steaming, seeping slush when not. Black ice windows, areas of ice that are so transparent the dark water below can be seen, could be five feet thick or they could be too weak to travel on.

At any point along the river the water level occasionally rises and the current eats away at the ice, reducing it to an unsafe thinness that could collapse under the sled. According to Frank Turner, conditions under any given section of ice can change within four to five hours.

When the river freezes, the ice is initially at one level. Then, below the ice, the water level drops as it's glacial sources in the mountains also freeze. Canyons of ice are formed when the ice, no longer supported by the water, collapses in the middle.

There are cracks, formed by changing surface pressures that are small enough to trap a dog's foot or large enough to swallow the entire dog. Some areas never freeze shut for one reason or another. They can be identified by a stationary fog during the day or the roar of the river current at night.

All of these hazards may be exposed by the north wind or disguised under dry, sandlike snow that is so coarse it can cut the dogs' feet and tear up the plastic runner-bottoms. On this treacherous surface, the Yukon Quest becomes like no other race on earth.

"The river itself was real jumbled ice and we had to run right on the bank," said Ed Salter in 1987, "It was just hundreds of miles of sidehills. And it was pretty tough, real hard on the teams."

Jim Reiter will remember the river by the ache in his ankles that he gets from leaning so hard, for so long as he rides his sled along the sides. "It all depends on the ice conditions," he says,"they put the trail in then the river drops over the next two weeks or so. Even when they broke the trail, the ice couldn't have been that stable so they really never did get out onto the river itself. I'd rather run the sidehills anyway than take a chance of getting wet."

Even after the trail has been set, the river surface can change. In 1986, Sonny Lindner was among a group of mushers who spent the night looking for the trail "We kept zig-zagging from one side of the river to the other. Two of the markers on the trail went right up to open leads on the river." During the night, the river had risen and eroded away the ice the mushers had crossed over just a few minutes earlier.

The mushers linger in Circle City, preparing physically and psychologically for the first long haul on the Yukon Quest: 180 miles upriver to Eagle. It is just a short section of the world's tenth longest river and it occasionally provides evidence of thousands of years of river travel by man, but it's recorded history is one of the shortest of the world's great waterways.

The Indians called it Yu Choo, "Great River," and it was the last major river in North America to be explored by Europeans. The Russians found the mouth of the river in 1834. The headwaters were discovered in 1840 but it wasn't until 1852 that the river was actually explored and mapped.

In the 1880s, prospectors, disillusioned by the dwindling number of valuable mineral finds further south, made their way into the Yukon River watershed. Small communities started popping up around areas where gold was found: 40-Mile in 1886. Circle in 1892. Dawson City in 1896.

The Yukon River was the highway connecting the interior gold fields of Alaska with the fabled Klondike in the central Yukon. It was the history of gold discoveries in the north and the postal service they spawned that caught Roger Williams' imagination in Whitehorse in 1981.

The mail carriers were the most frequent users of the trails on the river and, in winter, kept them clearly marked and broken. They drove massive freight sleds pulled by eight to 10 large powerful dogs, about twice the size of today's racing dog, hitched in single file. Occasionally the mail carriers took passengers, but the passenger didn't just ride. They had to run alongside, riding only when they needed a rest, to keep the sled as light as possible for the dogs.

It was a livelihood filled with risk. In 1901, a mail carrier waited patiently for an overdue sled to arrive at one cabin (cabins were built the length of the river to provide shelter). Finally, he headed upriver, thinking he might meet the delayed team. All he found was a hole in the ice with a fur hat lying beside it.

The last carriers on this stretch of the river were Adolphe and Charlie Biederman who handled the mail between Circle City and Eagle in the 1930s. They were mailmen not to be trifled with. Despite the fact the round trip took eight days, the mail always got through precisely on schedule, regardless of the weather or ice conditions.

But their time was running out. The airplane was becoming the mailman of the future for the remote communities and in 1940, the Biedermans lost their contract to Wien Air Alaska. That gradually became the fate of dog sled mail carriers over the next two decades and, in 1963, the final dog sled mail driver in Alaska retired.

For Ralph Tingey, an avid student of history, there is a feeling of Deja Vu, of having been there before. "I drove past rock walls I'd seen in a 1920 photo of an old time mail carrier on the Yukon River."

Overnight, the Arctic air mass has faltered. The cold is being gradually broken down by a slightly warmer block of air, pushing the temperatures up to about minus 10.

David Sawatzky tucks the last of his gear inside the sled bag and pulls the zipper tight. The dogs shiver with excitement and pull at their harness collars — they are ready to go and looking forward to getting back on the trail. However, there is none of the frantic excitement and lunging that took place in the starting chute in Fairbanks.

Sawatzky steps onto the runners at the back of the sled. "Hike!" he shouts. A jarring yank by the dogs, a push from the driver and the sled jerks loose from the hard packed snow and

Jack Hayden leaving Circle City, 1984.

moves past the other teams who perk up at the sudden activity. First into the checkpoint, he is the first to leave.

Gerald Riley doesn't look like he is in a rush, but he is next out an hour later. "My strategy is to stay light, travel fast and draw out the leaders." Within four hours, 14 drivers have pulled out of Circle City.

Bruce Lee isn't looking forward to the canyons of ice. "There's no life on the river in winter," he says. "It's just a frozen path with willow and spruce trees along the bank. It's the same scenery in one stretch as it is around the next corner. The dogs get bored. The pace slows down and they trudge along until they get to an open stretch where they can see something different. Then they perk up."

Race judge Ed Foran is more concerned with the logistical problems a stretch of trail like this could bring. "It is long and will separate teams. It's not racing from checkpoint to checkpoint any more. Some of the teams just hanging on with the front runners will start to fade away." The gap between the teams in front and back can stretch from hours to days and keeping track of all the teams will become more difficult.

While the trail skirts alongside the river for the first couple of miles, it swings inland through the Enchanted Forest before finally dropping onto the ice for the duration of the way. The short overland section earned that name in 1986.

That year, the teams battled their way through a snowstorm that just wouldn't stop, which forced the drivers to break trail for almost the entire 1,000 miles from Fairbanks to Whitehorse. The snow fell so heavily every day for two weeks that the trail filled in almost as fast as each individual sled could break its way through.

Jeff King, with blood stained ice hanging from his moustache (the blood came from the ice cutting into his upper lip), stumbled around feeding his dogs on the trail. "It's no longer the team that has the fastest dogs," he said to reporters, "It's by no means a race anymore. That ended when we hit the snow. We just went 25 miles and it's like we went 80."

For the first few miles out of Circle, the snowbound mushers also had to contend with a trail that the trailbreakers had somehow managed to snake through the trees. It became painfully obvious that a six-foot-long snow machine could go places that a dog team stretched out over 40 feet couldn't.

"We called that section The Enchanted Forest because it's almost impossible to drive dogs in there and live through the experience," said Joe May. The 50-year old former Iditarod champion (1980) had been lucky; only his sled bag had been damaged. King had splintered parts of his sled as he dodged around stumps and tried to squeeze between trees on the narrow trail.

Harry Sutherland lost it on a sharp turn; his sled spun then jammed sideways across the trail. Jon Rudolph was right behind him and couldn't get his dogs past the jack-knifed team. "There was a stump caught between his brake and runner. We needed a saw to cut the sled out."

Frank Turner couldn't believe how tight the corners were. "If you've got 10 or 12 dogs, the corners are too tough, too sharp. Your team almost starts coming back on itself. That's where you start getting dogs hung up on the neckline and start getting injuries. I don't know how else I can describe it. It's just a very narrow trail with trees all over the place. It wasn't made for teams to go through. There were trees literally stuck in the middle of the trail and you had no way around them."

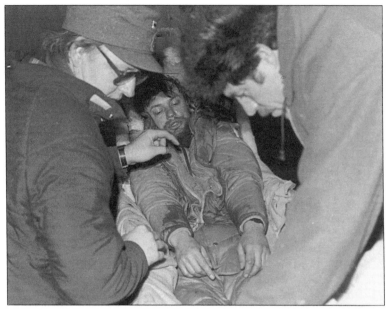

Ed Borden getting treatment at Circle City, 1986.

Bruce Johnson talked about U-turns so tight at the end, he could reach over and pat his lead dog on the head as it came up the other side of the bend. "It's a wonder there haven't been any dogs killed." A few dogs were hurt, and one was actually knocked unconscious in a collision with a tree.

Since that year, the trail has been gradually improved but it still features areas that make the teams work for any ground they may gain. And the hazards don't end after exiting the trees.

Ed Borden took it easy in '86 going through the trees and reached the river ice without too much damage. He took a short stop to feed the dogs, then kept on driving. The trail was rough; it was tossing the sled back and forth as the team passed through an area of rugged pack ice. Borden, balancing on the runners, went to step out to steady the sled and found his knee crushed between the 300-pound sled and a block of ice.

Some knocks hurt at first, without being serious. Borden gritted his teeth and waited for the agony to subside. But it didn't. He noticed the leg starting to get cold below the knee, and the pain was starting to physically wear him out. He dug in his brake, stopping the team, then hobbled forward to turn the team around to return to Circle City. Heading back, his hands started to swell, then to freeze.

When Don Glassburn met Borden's team, six hours later, just seven miles from Circle, Borden was semi-conscious. His arm was wrapped around the driving bow of his sled, but the rest of his body was dragging in the snow behind.

Glassburn loaded the injured musher onto his sled, tied the confused and frightened dogs to the back, then backtracked to a cabin occupied by Doug Dill. Dill piled Borden onto his snow machine and headed for town. The checkers at Circle City were startled to see a snowmobile come out of the darkness shortly after midnight.

"I need help," said Dill, "I have a musher with a broken leg in the sled."

"Sorry for the rough ride," he apologized to the injured musher.

"Hey, I don't even remember," mumbled Borden.

The next day Borden scratched. It was his final race. His smashed knee on the Yukon River was the second major crash within a couple of months for the musher who lived with the reality he may not be able to race again. Multiple Sclerosis can be aggravated by physical trauma and within two years he was bed-ridden by the disease.

A little further up the river, Dean Seibold and his team found a thin patch of ice in 1987 and dropped into three feet of water — not enough to drown them, but sufficient to be a threat at minus 50 degrees. As Siebold dried himself by a fire, the dogs dried themselves off by rolling in the snow. Snow in extremely cold temperatures tends to be very dry and acts like a sponge.

The long hours and rough trails start to wear the drivers out by this point in the race. Sleep becomes a rare commodity and what-ever shut-eye the mushers can grab is welcome. But sometimes those moments can come at the most inopportune times.

"I know one night I wanted to sleep," remembers Ed Salter, "And I didn't want to lie down. The thought of lying down in that temperature just didn't sit right even though I was really tired and I was almost sleeping standing up. I just grabbed the handle-bar and figured if I fell asleep I'd fall over on my dogs."

Ralph Tingey isn't in the habit of falling asleep on his sled, but there's one incident from the 1987 race he won't forget . . . or re-member.

"I fell asleep on the sled and I must have been asleep for a while. When I camped the next day with Dean Seibold he said, `Boy, wasn't that stretch of the Yukon back there horrible with that ice kind of sloping into that huge open hole?' I said, 'Dean, I fell asleep on the sled yesterday. What hole?' He says, 'There was this great big hole, with the river boiling through it, and there was all this side ice and it was really hard to negotiate.' I said, 'Oh.' "

Now, with the Arctic air mass collapsing around them, the warmer temperatures slow down the pace. The days are too warm for the dogs with their fur coats and the drivers travel mainly in the cooler night hours.

"I couldn't believe just how beautiful it was driving on the Yukon River with just polypropolene gloves in the moonlight, in the northern lights, in February," says Vern Halter.

David Sawatzky can't maintain his lead on the river. Kathy Swenson, Dave Monson and Bruce Lee pull ahead of him. Gerald Riley, the self-avowed hater of trail-breaking, is running his own distinct race a short distance behind them. While the others are systematically running four hours on and four hours off, Riley is blasting along non-stop for 12 or 16 hours, then resting for 12 to 16 hours. But he refuses to pull up with them, allowing them to set the pace and break the trail.

Some of the drivers will camp on the river all the way to Eagle, but most will stop at one or more of the cabins along the way. A few, like Ron Rosser, will stop at some of the lesser used locations. In 1986, he overnighted in a cabin owned by a German woodcarver, ate a meal of cookies and home-made beer at a small place occupied by a French Canadian woman and visited a hermit who lived in a teepee.

It was that year that all the mushers were forced off the ice and into the cabins along the river. Not much had gone right for the teams from the moment they left the starting chute. The snow had fallen relentlessly. The temperatures stayed cold. A blinding headwind was being funnelled down the river valley. A dozen drivers shared the lead, alternating the first place position.

Before the 1986 Yukon Quest, was over the drivers, many of them veterans of the Alaska mushing circuit, would call it one of the toughest races ever run.

Jon Rudolph remembers the time spent in the canyons that year. His voice sounds old as he recalls it: age not measured in years but by the experience of having been there. "People were falling off their sleds, they were so tired, but we kept going. No one wanted to be left out there. It was blowing so hard I couldn't see my own hands on the driving bow. We all moved like a train following a string of lights at night. When the leaders stopped, we all stopped. When the first light started moving again, we'd all get going again."

The '87 Quest featured a bitter cold that took its toll on the teams as temperatures got stuck around minus 50 and stayed there. Jon Gleason's hands and face were dry and splitting from frostbite. "I took off from Slavin cabin[1] and I got cold. I mean really cold." He pulled off the trail again a few miles further down at Biederman's cabin[2]. Inside the cabin, he felt the pins and needles of warm blood revitalizing the nerves in his frozen parts. The weird thing was that his tongue hurt too. "I was eating these M&M's and it was 50 below. I'm just shoving them into my mouth. I was so damn tired I should never have done that. I should have put them in my pocket, warmed them up, then ate them. I'm at Biederman's and my tongue starts to hurt. I'm trying to figure out, 'Geez, how come my tongue hurts? I haven't drank any hot soup or coffee.' All of a sudden I realize I've been eating all those M&M's and froze my damn tongue."

To live on the Yukon River is to step back in time — to an era when people didn't lock their doors, when a stranger was someone who used your cabin without your knowledge while you were gone and left you a fresh pile of split firewood as payment.

Swiss architect Peter Thomann, who will run the 1990 Yukon Quest, will be astounded at the inhabitants of the cabins who open their doors, sit back and let the mushers take complete possession of their home. "Sometimes they don't even know who we are. I'm amazed that sort of thing can happen."

The chili at Slavin's Cabin, manned today by the National arks Service, is second to none. In addition they offer hot coffee, stew, hot soup and freshly baked bread for the drivers and water for the dogs.

Biederman's cabin is abandoned for most of the year, but each February Mark and Laurie Richards travel 50 miles by dog sled from their own wilderness home to set up and operate a ham radio station there for the Quest organization. They provide food and shelter for the teams, then radio forward to the next checkpoint to let them know who's in and how they're doing.

For the first few years of the Quest it was occupied by a fellow called Woody Wilson. After offering hospitality for the first two years he was there, Wilson tried to capitalize on the mushers passing by in 1987. He set up a bed-and-breakfast for the teams. A room was $40 for the night. A bowl of soup was $5.00 and a bun was $3.50. Cash only please, no cheques or credit cards accepted. The mushers don't carry a lot of cash on the river and all passed him by. In '88, Wilson is gone and the cabin abandoned once again — except for the Richards.

Mike Sager at Trout Creek, about 40 miles from Eagle, is another regular stop. He's a fisherman, trapper and carver. The bannisters on his staircase to the second floor are hand carved from top to bottom. Here, the coffee's always on. The drivers are welcome to floor space if they want to sleep, and if they want conversation, Sager can't be described as the quiet type either.

"What an interesting guy," said Leroy Shank in 1987, "We were up most of the night talking with him and it was one of the most enjoyable parts of that section of trail."

Trout Creek is also the site of the most infamous outhouse on the trail. The outhouse is perched on the edge of a cliff, about 20 feet above the spot where the teams rest their dogs. At one time, the embankment in front of the outhouse must have been wide enough for a footpath, since the door looks out over the camping area below in the creek valley.

But the bank has eroded and the front door of the outhouse has disappeared. The only way into the small log-walled structure is through a hole in the back wall. The occupant then sits in full view of the other mushers. Not only can it be somewhat indiscreet, but it can also be downright embarrassing. David Sawatzky lost his balance in 1987 while crawling in from the back, fell out the front door and rolled down the embankment into the camping area.

Cabin fever has also reared its bizarre head. Isolation and low light levels in winter have odd effects on individuals and it's one of the reasons people do strange things after living for extended periods in the north.

In 1986, Ron Rosser and Frank Turner pulled into a cabin a few miles from Eagle about eight at night. There was one occupant — "a big, big man, about 230 pounds. Darrel was his name." said Turner. "He had hot chocolate for us and really made us feel welcome."

The two drivers pulled out again close to midnight, but the trail was blown in and the snow kept falling. They decided to turn back to the cabin to wait for some daylight to tackle the trail.

"We got back to the cabin, and all of a sudden", says Turner, "this guy just flips out. He wasn't going to let us back into the cabin. He started calling us all these names I've never heard before. I guess he had this macho thing that once we were gone, there was no turning back.

That's the only person I ever had any trouble with. Everyone else along the river is so happy to see you. They don't see a lot of people for a lot of months every year. . . and it's a really big thing for them."

Led by Kathy Swenson, the front teams start to open a gap between themselves and the rest of the pack. Swenson, Monson, Lee, Riley and Sawatzky start a push towards Eagle from Trout Creek. The trail is punchy from the heat (the trail is soft and the dogs' feet punch down into the snow), but it is faster than the crystallized snow of the previous two years.

The warmer temperatures also make cooking dog food a little easier. In '87, Swenson boiled some dog food for her team, but before the dogs could completely devour the hot food, it had frozen in the bottom of the pan.

In addition to marking the route and packing the trail, the trail-breakers have also provided some other aids along the river over the years, some of which have more value for the drivers than others.

Senley Yuill and Bill Cotter both remember a small sign on a portage just outside of Eagle in 1984. It had the standard crossed trail markers to warn the teams, but there was also a small sign nailed to a tree just a little further on. Just past the sign on the tree was a 15-foot embankment that dropped steeply down to the river.

"By the time you got to the sign to read it, half of your team was over the bank," said Yuill, "The sign said, `Check bank before going over,' but by then you were going whether you wanted to go or not."

Ahead of the teams, where the town of Eagle is perched on a level gravel bench above the Yukon, the residents watch and wait. With the exception of occasional static-filled reports from ham radio stations, there is only speculation about who is in front and when they will arrive.

The entire village of Eagle is involved in the Quest, either as volunteers or as supporters who come out at the ringing of the church bell, no matter what hour of the day or night it may be, to greet the teams. Only once will the bell not greet every musher who arrives: in 1990, the rope will be found frozen to the side of the church.

When access from the "outside" is limited to those who will travel the river, or land on the small airstrip, every visitor to the town is a welcome one. There is a special heart in the way the inhabitants of this collection of historical log cabins — hung with moose and caribou antlers and hides — and modern structures, put into their Quest participation.

The people that live here are a distinctively independent breed. They are here because they like the feeling of being distant from the giant urban centres and the society such metropolises spawn. It is about as far from the bright city lights as you can possibly get. The residents are rebels in their own right and are proud of their history of fighting government bureaucracy. Battling the government is almost an obsessive pastime in Eagle. Rarely does a year go by without a major dispute over one issue or another. They share a strong identity with the drivers on the river. Both are doing what they chose to do rather than something they have to do.

The weather here stinks for most of the winter. "The people at Eagle have a most commanding view of the river," describes resident Hudson Stuck, "But they pay for it." The wind normally whistles relentlessly around the snow encrusted collection of new and old buildings, and the mercury usually drops to the bottom of the thermometer and stays there for the winter.

But for some reason, this year it's different. Checkpoint worker John Borg is surprised at the light wind and warm temperatures. "This is the warmest Quest since the beginning. Usually, every year the mushers arrive with or ahead of a big snow. It'll be a pleasant change this year."

The residents take turns watching the foot of Eagle Bluff, watching at night for a tell-tale headlamp or during the day for anything that would change the whiteness of the snow around the base of Eagle Bluff. It is around the base of this massive buttress of rock, that juts out into the river about a half mile downstream from the town, that the first musher will appear.

Checking in at Eagle.

Standing and watching the river, volunteer Serge Waller is looking forward to the arrival of the first driver. For him, the Quest is another indicator of the end of winter and the coming of spring. "The Quest is a break in the monotony. Everyone looks forward to it and pitches in." Even the children share spotting duties.

Dusk is coming and still there's no sign. Radio signals from Biederman's, Mike Sager's place at Trout Creek or even from Dick Cook, just a few miles out of town at Miller's Camp, are being jammed by the effects of the aurora borealis on the atmosphere. But an incoming pilot reports seeing teams closing in on Eagle, well past Miller's Camp.

The gathering darkness is suddenly pierced by a small, sudden sharp spot of light on the river. "Team on the ice," shouts a voice. Another light, just minutes behind the first, appears in the distance. The church bell starts to clang and a crowd starts to gather near the small schoolhouse where the checkpoint is located. The light vanishes momentarily.

Whoever it is has reached the end of the trail on the ice and is now entering the trees. Now the light can be seen intermittently between the trees as the team creeps close until the whole team is illuminated by the spot light shining from the front of the schoolhouse.

The smiling tired eyes of Kathy Swenson drink in the scene of the applauding spectators. Her dogs stand wagging their tails, their tongues hanging out.

"How was it?" asks one bystander, as the checkers identify the mandatory items[3] on the sled and the veterinarians look over her dogs.

"Not bad," she replies, "yesterday I spun around on the ice in a circle for about 10 minutes while the wind blew. Trail's pretty punchy."

Dave Monson is the second headlamp. "We're a happy bunch of campers," he smiles in response to a deluge of questions about his strategy. "We only fight about who is the first to leave the campsite."

More lights on the river; more teams stream steadily into Eagle through the night. Some teams recently found overflow on the ice just outside of town and are soaked. Frank Turner has gone for a wild ride just a couple of miles out when his team smelled a wolf on the wind and bolted for a short distance. Gerald Riley pulls in silently, then parks his team in an isolated area away from the other drivers. His dogs look rested.

He is the subject of silent scrutiny from the other drivers. "He often travels just out of sight behind us and when he pulls in front, he turns out his headlamp so we can't see where he is," mutters Swenson. Riley simply smiles when he hears suggestions that he's playing "head games."

"Keeping other mushers guessing is one way a fast team can pull ahead of other teams of comparable abilities," he states.

In previous years, the trail beyond Eagle to Dawson City had continued along the Yukon River. But there is too much open water and rotten ice there this year. The trail has been re-routed overland. It goes up the mountain behind Eagle to American Summit, on top of the Dawson Range, then down the Forty-Mile River back to the Yukon River for the final few miles into Dawson.

There is relief that finally they are free of the canyons of ice. But there is apprehension, too: the route over American Summit is unknown to any of the drivers, trail conditions and prevailing winds are major unknowns. The memories of their most recent experiences above tree line, three days ago on Eagle Summit, are still fresh in their minds.

Footnotes

1 Slavin cabin, about halfway between Circle and Eagle, is named because former British Empire heavyweight boxing champion Frank Slavin was supposed to have lived there. Slavin quit the ring after he had been denied an opportunity to fight for the world championship in the 1890s and headed north to the Klondike Gold Rush. Arriving too late to stake a gold claim, he made a living with exhibition boxing bouts (against world wrestling champion Frank Gotch and Peter Jackson, a negro boxer denied a world title — shot by his skin colour despite being considered the greatest fighter to have ever donned the gloves), being a bouncer in the dance halls and cutting firewood during the summer to sell in the winter. This cabin was located on one of his wood lots.

2 This cabin was the summer home for the mail-carrying Biederman family in the 1930s. It was abandoned after they lost their mail contract in the 1940s.

3 The mandatory items include a pair of snowshoes, an axe, a sleeping bag, a map, a compass and promotional material, usually commemorative envelopes. With the exception of the promotional material, the mandatory items are the basic tools of survival in the wilderness.

SEEING THINGS

Broken. Alone on the trail. Days behind everyone else. His fingers and face frozen, ice preventing him from even untying his boots and no longer capable of motivating himself or his team, Michael Schwandt sank defeated into the snow on the Yukon River. He had long ago lost contact with any other stragglers in the 1986 Yukon Quest. His first shot at long distance racing now had the potential of turning into tragedy. He laid back and looked desperately to the heavens for divine inspiration.

The northern lights were there, dancing and weaving between the stars, hiding behind the mountains, then launching themselves across the sky in multi-coloured waves, drowning out the brightness of the stars themselves. A beautiful fantasy was played out across the universe above the motionless musher.

The very air sang to him, with the crackling hum of the northern lights, with the haunting whispers of winds shifting the snow softly across the ice. And when they stilled, in his mind, he could hear the trees in the forest take a deep silent breath in anticipation of what would be coming up next. He could smell the crispness of the cold in the air. It pierced cleanly and deep into his sinuses. Then he smelled the distinctive tang of dog breath as his team, lying beside him, watched their driver intently.

The assault on his senses penetrated into his world of dark despair and rejuvenated Michael Schwandt. He struggled to his feet. The dogs stood up, their tails wagging.

His fingers and face never really thawed out. He was always alone on the trail. He never stopped being tired, but he never gave up. Michael Schwandt completed the 1986 Quest, the toughest race ever run, arriving five days after the winner. He was almost three weeks on the trail.

For each driver the northern lights have a different meaning. For Schwandt, the lights turned potential disaster into personal triumph. Lorrina Mitchell views them as being a form of astral companion that watches over the teams as they travel.

"They seem like another living thing because they have motion and light. You're out there alone, and all of a sudden it's all right. You don't even feel the forty-below any more. You just say, 'Isn't that beautiful,' and when you see a falling star, that's really exciting."

Jennine Cathers echoes that sentiment. "Even when there's no one around, you get the feeling you're among friends."

Bill Cotter relates to them as part of the total experience of the trail. He remembers specifically a camp in the 1984 Quest he shared with Sonny Lindner, Jeff King and Joe Runyan. The four of them had lost the trail in the dark and decided to camp under an embankment, out of the wind.

"The stars were out. The northern lights were out dancing. We had a big bonfire and everybody hauled wood; fed the dogs and tried to keep warm all night. We talked about where we thought the trail was, how the dogs were doing. We swapped stories. It was one of the most fun times I ever had on the trail."

The northern lights are just part of the overpowering proximity of nature that captured Frank Turner's imagination.

"There's been times when you're out there and you're just by yourself. It almost becomes like a religious or spiritual experience, with the northern lights. A lot of people get religion out there. Not the church kind, I don't mean religion in that way. But it really is spiritual because you're so close to nature. You're so close to a total sense of being alive — there's nothing that transcends that. It's just an incredible, incredible feeling."

Not all the light shows are provided by nature. The drivers, after four or five sleepless days and nights on the trail, can provide much of their own inspiration and entertainment.

"Lots of hallucinations," says Jon Rudolph, sitting in his office two years after running his last Quest. He mimics the exhausted driver on the sled: "There's a checkpoint coming up. It's there. Yeah. It's there! It's coming up . . . there's no light there. It's not a light. What the hell was that?"

And again, reflecting from his chair, no longer on the trail, "It's scary . . . You say to yourself, 'I've got to get back to reality. I'm here on a dog team. How are the dogs doing? They're just going down the trail. There's nothing going on here; it's all in your head.' Then, just when you're back down again, you look up and you start drifting away again."

John Schandelmeier looks into the sky and sees only headlamps dancing in the dark. "You see all sorts of things when you're running on empty."

Ed Salter did a nosedive off his sled into the snow when he spotted a bear right beside his head. "It was just shadow. I started to laugh. Bears hibernate in winter." Marc Boily, an experienced long distance driver with three Iditarods and one Quest under his belt, watched the trees move, marching alongside the river. Dave Monson hears people singing and yelling. At night, patches of willow trees turn into herds of caribou. Stationary tree stumps become wolves racing alongside the trail.

Jon Gleason suddenly came under attack from a wave of flying swords and spears. "I'm ducking and weaving and bopping and I end up falling off the dang dog sled." Another time he spotted his daughter Shayne riding on the back of Snowball, one of his dogs. "What are you doing out here?" he asked, "You're supposed to be home with your mother."

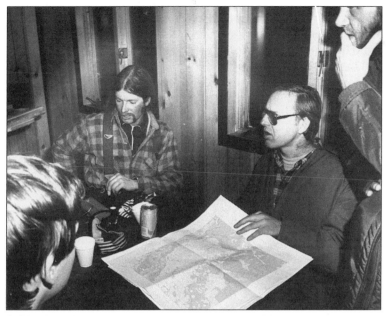

Trail briefing in Eagle for Sonny Lindner from Leo Oleson (R), 1984.

Confusion can result when the musher suddenly sees his dogs facing the sled and running backwards down the trail. The heart can momentarily stop when they vanish into black holes in the ice, only to miraculously reappear on the other side, running as if nothing had happened.

In 1984 Harry Sutherland spotted someone sitting on his brush-bow. "This guy was in a T-shirt and he was riding in front of my sled, smoking a cigar, drinking a Coke and blowing smoke rings at me. There he was, then he'd go away when I realized it was an hallucination, then he'd come back again." Occasionally, his passenger would ask a question: about the dogs, about philosophy, whatever. And Sutherland would respond. It wasn't his only vision on the trail, but the fact that he answered made it memorable.

Frank Turner once saw Jon Rudolph standing by his sled puffing on a pipe, but there were no sled tracks in the snow leading out to the sled and Rudolph, in reality, was miles away. Besides that, he doesn't smoke a pipe.

Not all drivers are subject to the scenarios the exhausted mind can conjure, but they are all aware of it. Joe Runyan uses a disciplined feeding-running schedule to keep his mind occupied and prevent himself from falling subject to the phenomenon. He even wears two watches, in case one breaks, to ensure he doesn't break from the pattern.

Lorrina Mitchell changes booties more often, stops a little more than usual and snacks the dogs. While travelling, she mentally re-designs the kitchen pantry in her new house or resolves never to put herself through this kind of stupidity again. Next year, just short races. When that line of daydreaming runs dry, she sings to the dogs:

Mush along little doggies
Mush along there well
Cause it's your misfortune
And none of my own
You know that you have to
Mush a thousand miles home."

The average dog team will trot between six and ten miles per hour. It's not the kind of speed where the mushers need to focus solely on steering, so they have to do something. A few, like Mitchell, sing to their teams. Others chat incessantly to them. "John Schandelmeier talks to his dogs," says Gleason, "You can hear him coming a mile away."

The biggest thrill for people like Senley Yuill is to sit on the back of the sled in silence and listen to the music in the patter of the paws on the crisp snow, the muffled thunder of the runners on the snow and the panting of the dogs. "It's so peaceful of a sound — like a quiet chair. It's got to be the most peaceful way to travel on earth."

It is into this world of inspirational light-shows, half-true fantasies and peaceful tranquility that Dave Monson enters when he hitches up under a partially full moon and pulls out of Eagle in the early hours of the morning. Bruce Lee and Kathy Swenson are just minutes behind.

On this portion of the trail everyone is a rookie. None of the drivers have ever run up the Taylor Highway (a summer-only road into Eagle), to American Summit and over the top of the Dawson Range of mountains. The ascent is a constant steady grind of 15 miles up the side of a sheltered valley. On top, they

124   YUKON CHALLENGE

Jerry Riley crossing American Summit, 1988.

pass over a seven mile stretch from one tree line to the other before starting to descend on the Top of the World Highway, a summer-only road from Dawson to Tetlin Junction. The top, according to the trail breakers, is notorious for winds and white-outs. The snow is hard packed by the wind and there are lots of drifts.

"It was every bit as wicked as Eagle Summit," says Jim Reiter, "I could see the country and where the wind had blown, the drifts that were in there. And it's a long way across there. At least on Eagle Summit, you could crawl your way across if you had to. This one here, you could wander around up there for a long time."

The wind has done its work on the few trees up that high. Over the years they have twisted and contorted themselves into the shapes that best protect against the harsh environment. In the light from the drivers' headlamps, the hoar-frost covered branches look as if someone had shattered the fragile darkness into a thousand cracks — deformed, pure-white spider webs spread over a velvet black background.

"You swear that these things come alive," describes Turner, "That they've got their own life when nobody else is around. They're only frozen when somebody's there to look at them."

Monson pulls up from the Taylor Highway and breaks onto the open summit. There is no wind tonight. There are no clouds in the sky. He shuts off his headlamp and lets his leaders take command. All around him he can see the wilderness surrealistically illuminated by the pale reflections of the stars and moon off the snow.

"It was so beautiful. The stars and moon were out. You were up on these vistas that you could see forever. You could see the teams way behind you, and you could look ahead and see where you needed to go. And the team was travelling along really well. And you were just enjoying the fact that you were out here in the wilderness doing something you had prepared yourself for all year."

It doesn't take long for Monson and the other leaders to clear the top and start down. And it isn't far past the tree line where the trail turns sharply off the Top of the World Highway and drops onto the Fortymile River. The trail snakes through narrow canyons in the river's upper reaches before widening into a substantial valley which takes them back to the Yukon River just 50 miles from the Dawson City checkpoint.

Several cabins line the narrow concourse. One of them, owned by '85 Quest veteran Dave Likins, has a lamp in the window to signal the drivers that here they can stop to feed their dogs, have a coffee, a bite to eat or just warm up.

Monson pulls up for a rest. Somewhere along the summit he has twisted his arm and he is finding it hard to hang onto the sled. Likins helps him wrap a bandage around it. Swenson turns up 20 minutes later; Bruce Lee is a half hour behind her. The three of them park, waiting for daylight and watching the trail behind. Around them, beneath the snow, lay the remains of the first of the major gold rushes that opened the interior of Alaska and the Yukon.

It was in 1886 that two brothers, Frank and Henry Madison ventured up the river and discovered gold. They called the river the Fortymile because it was believed to have been that far from Fort Reliance, a trading post further down the Yukon River. The town that grew to service the rush of miners to the area took on the same name as the river. Eventually it included a trading post and storage sheds, an opera house, six saloons and a multitude of sod-roof cabins, located where the Fortymile met the Yukon.

In addition to being the first of the gold rushes, it was also the most important in the development of the unique mining techniques and technology that came to be used in the north.It was here that the miners first encountered the difficulties of digging into permafrost: muck and gravel permanently frozen as hard as rock. They solved the problem by building fires at the bottoms of their mine shafts, then excavating the melted materials, which were mainly in the form of a soupy mud. The knowledge acquired in Fortymile was effectively applied later in the Klondike, Circle District, Fairbanks and Nome gold strikes.

When gold was discovered a few miles upstream in 1896, in the Klondike River Valley, most of the miners left Fortymile. But a few miners remained to scrape a living from the ground and it wasn't until 1958 that the original townsite was totally abandoned. Modern mining techniques revived interest in the area in the 1970s and there are still several individual operators, like Likins, profitably working the old river bed and the bench claims on the hills above.

Dawn comes. The three leaders can see a storm developing on the mountain behind them. As Monson and Swenson pack up to leave, Gerry Riley rolls through the yard, gives them a quick look and keeps on going. His brief appearance rattles the two drivers.

"At that point," says Monson, "It was kind of scary because I didn't know why his dogs were doing so good. The reason they were doing so good was because he was compelling a superior performance from them."

A game of cat-and-mouse starts to develop among the front four teams. They drive, then stop and wait to see who will take the initiative. Monson is the first to cross the border into Canada, 30 miles from Likins's cabin. Swenson is a few hundred yards behind; Riley and Lee are about two miles back of her.

Above and behind them, a wind starts to blow on top of the summit. "It was all windblown. Nothing on top so you can't stop and it was getting windy," describes Reiter, "Storm was coming. Tom Randall was right behind me and he ran through part of it. He had to hole up right after he got across."

The storm creates an even greater disparity between the teams up front and the rest of the pack which had managed to stay relatively close until now. Hampered by the winds and not knowing exactly where to look for the trail in the reduced visibility, the teams on the summit slow down. But they do not have to war with the weather as they did on Eagle Summit. The four teams up front stop to see if there is any one else in the hunt. "We stayed there for five hours and nobody else showed up," says Monson, "So at that point we'd already had a five hour rest and took off before anyone else turned up. That established the front pack right there. There were four teams. Those were the people you were going to be competing against."

"We've been together long enough to know what the others can do," summarizes Lee, "Now we took a hard look at our strong and weak points and try to figure out a plan that will eventually put us in front." But Lee knows his limitations. Looking at the other three teams, he smiles. "I'm keeping up. But I'm just travelling in their wake."

They pull out and, a few hours later, drop onto the Yukon River and turn south towards Dawson. This is Percy DeWolfe country.

The legendary mailman, who ran this trail by dog sled between Eagle and Dawson for three decades, was honoured in two countries for his single-minded determination that a job worth doing, was worth doing well.

DeWolfe, nicknamed the Iron Man of the Yukon, broke through the ice just below the mouth of the Fortymile. DeWolfe jumped free of the sled, then, realizing he couldn't save the team, leaped back and grabbed the mail bag. Throwing the mail onto the ice, he launched himself to safety just as the dogs and sled vanished under the black surface of the water beneath the ice. Picking himself up, he retrieved the mail and continued on foot the final 70 miles to Eagle.

None of the front four lose their teams through the ice at the mouth of the Fortymile, but in '89 all six lead teams will break through in separate incidents and find themselves partially immersed in the river.

Jeff King will sink to his armpits. "I was hanging onto my sled with one hand and paddling with the other. I couldn't touch bottom." He will pull himself out along the gang line, then help the dogs pull the sled free. There is a trapper's cabin close by that he will head for after getting onto secure ice. "My clothes froze up. I couldn't bend at the middle when I got there."

Gerry Riley will be standing on the trail close to where Kate Persons breaks through. "When she went through I grabbed her leader and gave the hardest pull I could. But the ice just kept breaking." With Riley pulling and Persons windmilling her legs on top of the broken ice and water, they will shift the sled to firmer footings. "She couldn't get her mukluks off," says Riley, "So I yanked and yanked and yanked. When we got them off I put one of her feet in my coat next to my skin to warm it up."

Breaking through isn't the only way the Yukon River threatens to swallow teams. Open leads also pose a threat, especially at night. Crossing a glaciated section just outside of Dawson City in 1985, Bill Cotter could hear a loud roar similar to the thunder created by falling water at Niagara Falls, but couldn't see anything in the dark. He turned his headlamp on and found his dogs trotting complacently just inches away from an open hole in the ice through which the river water was boiling up.

The biggest problem with open leads that can't be bypassed by going overland, is that the trail to go past them often is put on a sidehill just above. The trailbreaker sets the track 15 feet up from the hole, but as each team passes, the sleds cut the track a little lower down the hill and closer to the water. By the time the slowest teams approach, the trail can be right on the hole's edge. Only by tipping the sled and using the edge of the runner to direct the sled uphill can the driver avert disaster.

In 1984, Frank Turner didn't have any trouble with water, but encountered problems with all the things that had floated in it before it froze. He had bruised his hip in a collision with a log sticking out of the ice, broken his glasses and damaged part of his sled banging against pack ice. Now he had discovered his headlamp wasn't working and he was running out of dog booties.

"So what I would do is, as I went along, I would pick up dog booties along the way. Well, it was getting dark and I could see on the trail, there was a bootie up there. It was on the right side of the sled. So I slung my sled over to the side and I went down to pick it up . . . and it wasn't a bootie after all. It was a piece of dog shit. I said to myself, 'This has got to be the absolute end. There's nothing else that can possibly happen to me now.' "

The environment along the river is reminiscent of Eagle Summit and is just as unpredictable. While John Mitchell complains about the heat in 1985 — "It was so hot it was like being in

Hawaii. Every time I stopped to rest, my dogs dug caves in the snow to try and cool off," — Jon Rudolph remembers the snow storm in 1986.

"You couldn't see the next guy in front or behind you. You couldn't even see your dogs. But I knew there was a team less than 20 seconds ahead of me. His runner marks and everything else were completely wiped out. You'd all stop and someone changed the lead and you're supposed to get going. And you're yelling at the guy in front of you and he's sound asleep standing there. You had to go by and give him a kick and he'd wake up and off we go."

High clouds and light south winds are keeping temperatures just below freezing this year: perfect driving weather for teams who seek a fast time. On the river, the four drivers are using the packed trails to manoeuver for a psychological advantage.

Monson continues to lead until about 15 miles from Dawson when he stops to snack his dogs. Swenson and Lee have dropped back far enough that the bends in the river hide them from sight. Riley is right behind. He pulls over and snacks his team as well.

"How far is Dawson?" asks Riley.

"I don't really know," replies Monson. The two watch their dogs chew for a moment.

"Tell you what," suggests Riley, "I'll take over the lead and break trail for a while." Tired of being tailgated, Monson agrees. He had offered Riley the lead before, but breaking trail isn't the older musher's favorite task and he declined.

Riley feels that now might be the time to deflate Monson a little by beating him into Dawson City and winning the four ounces of gold that awaits the first arrival at the halfway point of the race. Riley takes off and opens a substantial gap quickly, but as he vanishes from sight a mile or so ahead, Monson has a change of heart. "I've been breaking trail now for 200 miles, why should I let him get into Dawson ahead of me?"

Riley continues to drive his team, confident he is on his way to an advantage. Monson gradually accelerates his pace, picking it up bit by bit. The difference between them starts to shrink. A couple of miles outside of Dawson, passing Moosehide Indian Village, his quarry comes within sight.

"He saw that I was catching him and that's when he really started kicking in, running and kicking and really trying to get his dogs going. But by that point my dogs were in a speed and it was

YUKON CHALLENGE

faster than he was going. Finally I caught him, gave the dogs the command to pass and really picked them up then and just thumped away from him just to get rid of him. I think for him that was probably the most demoralizing point of the race, because until then it had been his impression that he was faster than me."

Monson cuts it close. The welcoming wail of the Dawson City Fire Department siren greets him just eight minutes ahead of Riley. He is still in front of the two-story log tourism information centre, where the checkpoint is located, when Riley arrives.

The late charge, while successful, has both Monson and Riley concerned. The dogs look tired as they patiently wait for the formalities to end so they can find some straw and go to sleep. Even though they have a 36-hour stop awaiting them, it will only be when they get back on the trail that the question of how fast their teams can bounce back will be answered.

"I hope four ounces of gold doesn't end up costing me $20,000," says Monson, "That last push took something out of my dogs." The gold wasn't the reason for the finishing kick, he explains, "Coming in first was a question of honor."

Swenson pulls in two hours later. Her dogs look perky as they lope up the bank off the river. "I didn't want to get suckered into racing, so I stopped on the river to rest my dogs when Monson and Riley took off," she smiles confidently. "Now my dogs are fine and theirs are so tired they practically had to walk to town."

Bruce Lee's reason for falling back is sitting in his sled basket. One of his dogs injured a foot about 30 miles out of Dawson City. The extra weight and reduced pulling power has slowed him down. He is an hour behind Swenson, his dogs are sick, and he looks depressed.

Behind them Rick Atkinson and Dave Sawatzky have closed the gap a little, but aren't really within striking distance. It appears, barring any unforeseen catastrophe, that only three contenders remain in the race. These three are sleeping in Dawson City while the rest of the field struggles on, stretched out along the river and through the mountains as far back as Eagle where six teams have not yet arrived.

PARIS OF
THE NORTH

Dawson City has been the welcome sight at the end of the trail for weary travellers in the Yukon for 90 years.

It was the final destination for those 40,000 dreamers who arrived from the four corners of the earth to seek Klondike gold in 1898[1]. They laboured by foot over mountains and sailed in handbuilt boats and rafts across lakes and down rivers to catch a glimpse of the distinctive gravel scar[2] in the mountainside above the city that became known as The Paris of the North: the largest metropolis on the North American continent north of San Francisco and west of Winnipeg.

At its peak, Dawson City had a waterfront crowded with warehouses, streets packed with a bevy of saloons and dance halls, a hospital, several churches, a police detachment, an opera house, a multitude of restaurants, hotels and barbershops and no shortage of brothels. But even as it grew, it was dying. Like any gold rush boom town, it was destined to disappear when the gold was gone.

Less than 1,000 permanent residents now occupy the once-proud city which stands on the confluence of one of the world's greatest rivers (the Yukon) and one of its most famous (the Klondike).

The dog mushers, nearing the end of almost two full days spent driving through the snow from Eagle, are grateful to arrive. From the Yukon River, they climb into the city via the ice bridge — a strip of the river that has been reinforced by adding extra water on top of the ice to support the weight of heavy vehicles - then run along Front Street to stop by the Tourism Information Centre.

Once checked in, they turn around and return to the river, to cross it to a government campground on the opposite riverbank. In the summer, it is home for tourists' tents, trailers, campers and recreation vehicles. In winter, it is empty except when the Yukon Quest is in town.

And at that time, winterized Dawson warms up. The inhabitants, who hibernate indoors for much of the cold period, roll out to greet the teams. They open their homes, their hearts and Diamond Tooth Gerties — at one time, Canada's only legal gambling casino. These

YUKON CHALLENGE

visitors are only here until the lure of gold, this time at the finish line in Whitehorse, takes them away again. But while the teams are here, it's a good excuse to hold a party and the residents are determined to enjoy themselves. Dawson stands apart from the other checkpoints on the Quest for two reasons. First, this is the site of a mandatory 36-hour rest period for the teams. Other than a four-hour veterinarians' check at the final checkpoint before the finish line, it is the only required stop in the race. And secondly, this is the only spot on the entire trail where the mushers are permitted outside help in tending to the dogs and repairing the sled or equipment.

It's a nice feeling to arrive in the campground on the Yukon River. "Your handler takes over," said Jon Rudolph, "And you just dissolve from the race for 10 or 12 hours. You usually don't sleep very good. You go to sleep, but you're tense all the time. You wake up asking, 'Where are the dogs?' 'What am I doing in bed?' and 'Where am I?' Then you realize you're on your break and you don't really have to worry."

Just simple everyday activities, like taking a bath or doing laundry, become almost unbearable luxuries. "This is pretty comfortable. I mean, THIS IS NICE. And you start thinking about all the horror shows that have happened out on the trail and the misery you went through. You don't really look forward to getting back out there again."

"The 36 hours in Dawson is the fastest 36 hours you'll ever spend in your entire life," says Lorrina Mitchell, "You spend half the time sleeping and the other half is spent checking your dogs, giving your handler orders, working on the sled, lightening up your load. I always start the race with everything and the kitchen sink in the sled. Then, as the race progresses, you see what extra weight you can drop."

Jim Reiter won't even see his dogs from the moment he arrives until the moment he leaves. "Debbie met me and just took over the dogs. Says to me, 'I don't want to see you over at the dog yard until you're ready to go. Just stay away from them. They're tired of looking at you. You're tired of looking at them. Just let me baby them a little bit.' I slept quite a bit. Walked around town, visited, had a beer and went shopping for things that I'd either lost on the trail or had decided I needed."

Dawson is where the frustration of not being able to do anything and the nightmare of waiting ends for the handlers. For the first time since the race started, they can actively get involved. And for the

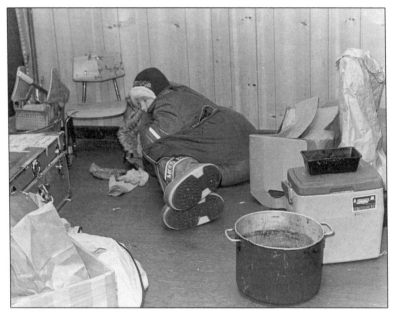

Grabbing a moment's sleep when you can, 1986.

next 36 hours they know exactly where their driver is and what he or she is doing.

While Dave Monson rests, his handler Nate Gray manages only 20 minutes of sleep. And he pays a price for it. "I fell asleep on a tree stump with my coat sleeve pushed up and my foot a little too close to the fire." His leg is burned and his wrist freezes. For the rest of the 36 hours Gray repairs equipment, mends the sled, applies foot medicine to the dogs (and puts the same stuff on his burned leg), walks them so they won't stiffen up too much, feeds them and waters them.

It is a thankless job for the 20-year-old native of Connecticut who flew north four months earlier specifically to do this job. It isn't the money that keeps him going; he makes only $50 per week plus room and board. It's a lust for adventure and a love for the dogs. When the racing season is over he will either return home, his desire for excitement satisfied, or he will stay in Alaska — another cheechako (newcomer from the outside) who, feeling the south too crowded and overdeveloped, is incurably enchanted by the wide open spaces and pure air.

YUKON CHALLENGE

"Mushers trust handlers with their lives and their dogs," said Bob English, a veteran of the 1984 Quest and a handler for Frank Turner in 1985, "They also depend on them mentally for a hug or a kick in the rear, whatever is needed."

"Handling lets me travel and spend the winter out in the bush without having to invest money in a dog team myself," explains Rick Atkinson's handler Don Schmuckal.

Gordie Mitchell has finally had it with long-distance racing. Lorrina takes more than two days to make the trip from Eagle, almost a half day slower than the average time over that distance. She has no real problems, the team is simply moving slower than they expected. But the emotional stress is finally too much for him. The fun is gone and the waiting game has turned into a nightmare of not being able to sleep or eat because the worry keeps his stomach upset and his imagination racing.

Gordie announces Lorrina's retirement to her when she arrives. "This is the last time we're going to do this," he states. She nods in agreement. This will be her final long-distance race, but it's not over yet. She heads for a bed while Gordie takes the team into the dog lot for their rest.

Mary Sheilds also trots in after an extended time on the trail. She'll finish this one, but this is it. While dog mushing will still be the centrepiece of her life, she won't race the thousand milers any more.

There are still a few teams out on the river. Tom Randall hasn't made it in yet and he hasn't been seen by anyone for the past 18 hours. His wife and handler Elsie Wain is playing it cool on the outside, but it's just a façade.

"The only thing I'm worried about is if something happened," she says, "I mean, we're sitting around laughing and joking about them partying on the trail—but it would be awful if he was hurt... But I vary between that fear and the urge to kill him when he gets here." Randall is spotted a few hours later, mushing along slowly but in no trouble, just a few miles out of Dawson.

While most of the worrying is done at the checkpoint in town and much of the work is done over at the dog lot across the river, there is one more spot where the handlers will spend a fair amount of their time.

A small workshop in the middle of town is turned into a dog sled hospital. Here the handlers replace with new pieces, the parts of the sled that were broken and temporarily repaired on the trail. One sled gets a new brushbow. Another needs several bolts replaced

Sled repair shop in Dawson City, 1987.

that broke due to a slight flaw in the sled design. Broken stanchions, ripped sled bags and damaged or heavily worn runners are the most prevalent injuries dealt with.

With dogs and sleds being tended to, the drivers have an opportunity to take care of themselves for a change. The race wreaks havoc with their bodies as they struggle through snow drifts, fight with the sleds on sidehills or run into open water. The mushers perspire and their clothes get wet from the inside. The snow and water soaks them from outside.

They are seldom, if ever, dry in the sub-zero temperatures and frigid winds. Thin sheets of ice form between layers of clothes and the insulating qualities of the material are eroded away. Denied the warmth of the clothing, the body gradually loses its ability to heat itself. The cold penetrates so deeply that neither hot food nor fire can relieve the aching bones.

It's common knowledge that most of the body's heat is lost through the extremities such as the hands, head and feet. The feet are the most vulnerable and a great deal of attention has been paid to taking care of them on the trail.

Some mushers wear mukluks with a foam insert. Dry, they are warm and comfortable, even at 60 below. Wet, the musher's toes

Hot feet in the cold snow, cure for bad feet.

and heels can freeze in minutes. They are also soft and provide no protection against bangs and bruises from kicking or stepping on chunks of ice or tree stumps.

Bunny boots, heavily insulated waterproof rubber and canvas boots with a steel shank supported sole, are still the most popular with the drivers. They are warm at any temperature, provide sufficient protection and function equally well in wet and dry conditions, yet they are the root of a lot of problems. Feet perspire and a boot that won't let water in, also won't let it out. The feet stay constantly wet, turning into prunes, then becoming hamburger.

The constant standing, walking and running also exacts a toll. Pain is the price the driver must pay to have warm feet.

"My feet hurt so much," said Senley Yuill in 1984, "I don't know if they're cold or not."

"You lose the feeling in them," says Mitchell, "You know they're not frozen. They're just desensitized."

Jon Gleason started out with mukluks in 1987, but when they got wet he switched to bunny boots. "Every bit of skin on the bottom of my feet—all that callus you build up over 40 years—came off. I had brand new feet, like the day I was born. It was like walking on hot coals all the time."

Dave Monson has a trick he learned from a mountain climber in Alaska to give his feet some relief. "If you take off your bunny boots every night and stick your feet in the snow for 10 minutes, it slams your pores shut and helps your feet. Keeps them from becoming tender. And your feet are so hot, they don't really freeze no matter how cold it is. You don't want to meditate for four hours, but you can certainly stand it for 10 minutes."

Cold weather head gear usually consists of hats made from wolf, fox or beaver pelts, since there are few insulators that can compare with the natural hide of an animal. The fur is inside the hat with a woollen felt on the outside. It has a flap, that can be folded up in warmer weather, to cover the back of the neck and the ears. When it's very windy or extremely cold, the mushers pull up the hood of their parka with fur trim around the facial opening. A light cotton or wool toque suffices during warm spells.

The mushers' mitts are usually made with fur backs and thick leather palms. Inside the mitts, they wear a light glove that enables them to keep their fingers relatively warm, yet flexible enough to be able to feed the dogs and work on the trail. The danger of forgetting their big mitts when they've reached the point of exhaustion is solved by use of an 'idiot-string' (a string attached to both gloves and looped around the individual's neck).

Just as there has been an evolution towards high efficiency in dog breeding, camping equipment and sleds, there has been progress in the clothes worn by the drivers. Working on improving the insulating quality and the practicality of the clothes is the goal of Shari Tingey, one of just a few clothing designers and manufacturers who are working in the field of producing custom winter wear for drivers.

After designing skiing and mountaineering clothes for 18 years in Wyoming, she found a new challenge when her husband Ralph moved to Alaska and started running dogs. The clothes she had designed for his mountaineering activities just didn't work for his activities as a dog musher. Just the flexibility required in the pants to enable him to bend over while tending to the dogs or pushing off from the back of the sled was something she had never had to plan for previously.

So out came the drawing board and up went the sewing machine. "My love was always to try to make clothes that just really worked well for whatever situation you were going to be in, rather than designing a general all-purpose jacket. Nothing I'd done before suited Ralph for running dogs. Then a few people came when they learned I made clothes and asked me to make coats for these long distance races and that sort of got my interest going."

At that time most mushers wore a material called Venteel, a tight woven cotton material. It was tough, but it absorbed water and perspiration and eventually lost its insulating qualities. They like wool too, which stays warm when wet, but it is extremely heavy. Snowmobile suits are another option, but they are only good for short stays in the cold. Down parkas are effective when dry, but lose their warmth when wet. Frank Turner discovered another short-coming of the down parka in 1984 when he tried drying his out over his campstove.

"The shell in my jacket was really wet from perspiration and we camped off the side of the trail. We didn't light a fire. I just had my stove so I hung my jacket over the back of my sled and the snowshoes I stuck in the ground. I put my MSR stove under the parka and we were sitting and talking on the sled, when all of a sudden I heard this 'Whoomp!' We looked around and there's nothing but feathers floating through the air. I found out down is a very combustible ... extremely combustible material. I've never used down since."

Tingey, and other designers, turned to manmade materials such as Gortex, Thinsulate and Thermalite. They were lighter, wind-proof, just as warm and more practical. The designers also stuck strictly to the concept of ensuring each piece of clothing was as uncomplicated as they could make it.

"You're talking about 65 below [Fahrenheit], high winds and the individual inside that parka is sweating because they're working hard. You want this stuff to work. You've got to make it the simplest thing you can come up with — you've got to get rid of anything that can screw up."

But like anything else in a period of rapid technological change, each suit that came off her sewing machine was different from the one that preceded it. And each driver had personal preferences.

"I started out with the zippers changing four or five times. Then some people didn't want zippers. Gators inside the legs for mushers who use bunny boots rather than mukluks, snap-on hoods, hoods permanently attached. I'd say the first 15 coats I made changed every single time."

For Tingey, what started out as a quest for the perfect winter suit, turned into the evolution of two winter suits in one: a bib-style pair of pants (which allow for bending over to feed the dogs) and a long parka overtop.

Her husband, Ralph, tends to feel the cold, but wearing both pieces of her coat, he can sleep on top of the snow without a sleeping bag and not get a chill. Dennis Kogl, on the other hand, usually wears only one of the pieces because he doesn't get cold.

For the drivers, clothes are not just a form of protection from the environment, they are often the butt of off-beat humour. Bruce Johnson and Jon Rudolph spent a few slap-happy hours, parked below the Black Hills south of Dawson City in 1985, talking about Joe May, who was one of the first to wear the new high-tech mushing suits.

"Did you see Joe," said Johnson, "with his clean red suit at the start line? Yesterday I looked at it and it's all covered with dog shit. It's got burn holes in it from the fires and it's all ripped up."

Then they laughed so hard that Johnson's hat fell off his head and landed in the dog food. He retrieved the dripping headgear from the pot and replaced it on his head. Then they started to laugh again at the liquid freezing in icicles hanging from his hat around his head.

The musher's stomach takes the worst abuse of any part of the body: not because the drivers eat bad food, but just because they don't eat enough. Most of them carry freeze-dried foods that are easily and quickly cooked in boiling water. Pizza or hot dogs warmed up in a fry pan over the stove or a fire are big favourites. Food with fats in them, like salami sausages, or with sugar for instant energy, like honey or chocolate, are popular snack items. Turkey, chicken and beans are avoided in warm weather because of the danger of salmonella.

Rookie mushers will suffer the most. In their first few races, they tend to lose a lot of weight on the trail, but when they have less waistline and more races under their belt, the diet starts to improve.

Harry Sutherland is one of the veterans of the racing circuit. He eats "surf and turf" (lobster tails and steak) on the trail although it is fairly primitive — there's no wine or silverware. Compare that to the unappetizing bags of brown "glop" that Eric Buetow, 1986 President of Yukon Quest International, dropped into pots of boiling water during his first Quest in 1985. What exactly he was eating nobody ever found out for sure since no one else wanted to eat it.

Sometimes fast food outlets come in handy. Frank Turner left his pre-cooked and pre-packaged human food for the 1984 race on his front porch when he drove off to Fairbanks, so he had to find a substitute and find one quickly.

"So I went to Burger King, explained the situation, and the manager said, 'Come back in an hour.' I went back and he had 25 patties stacked there. I said, 'This is great, but do you think I can get some buns too?' And he said, 'Your dogs eat buns too?' They had the pickle on them and everything and all the way to the first checkpoint I had these frozen burgers just clanging around against each other. I finally cleaned them out because I couldn't eat them anymore. Once they got frozen, they just weren't any good any more."

Constantly perspiring and exhaling moisture into the cold, dry air while not drinking regularly or enough can dehydrate a musher. The first symptoms of dehydration are a loss of concentration and the tendency to get chills easily. The musher can check for dehydration easily enough by checking the color of their own urine. If it's a rusty color, it's time to be concerned about drinking habits.

"I can remember saying to Sonny Lindner (in 1986), 'God I'm so cold. What's the temperature?' And he says, '34 degrees. Plus 34 degrees.' Why am I so cold? Then I remember I've got a half gallon thermos that I've been carrying for 24 hours. I haven't taken a drink in 24 hours," said Harry Sutherland, "You're always checking the dogs' urine, every time the dog takes a leak you're looking to see what color his urine is so you can tell how much water he needs. And I got to looking at my own and I'm worse than the dogs."

Water and coffee are the two prime sources of liquid. Gatorade or Jolt (a soft drink with a kick to it) is used to give a shot of instant energy and to replace fluids. While a beer or two at the checkpoints isn't uncommon, alcohol is rare.

Kathy Swenson carries a little bottle of liqueur to give her coffee a little bite and Lorrina Mitchell admits to carrying a small flask "to help me shut down when I'm over-tired. One sip of alcohol will relax all the nerves in your body, then you can go to sleep."

Driving the team isn't just a matter of sitting back on the runners and letting the dogs do all the work. The musher, like the dogs, is constantly working and needs to have the ability to bounce back after a week or so of pushing themselves to the limit. It takes powerful arms to manhandle the three to four hundred pound sled while it's moving across a sidehill or skidding off a packed trail into deep snow. A strong back is needed for the lifting and for the hours that are spent bent over feeding the dogs or tending to their feet.

A well-conditioned heart and cardiovascular system are vital. Something as simple as having a cold wind blow in your face can raise blood pressure significantly. Any emergency situation, such as the team refusing to run in the face of a storm or getting away from the driver, causes extra physical and emotional stress.

The mushers' legs are usually very solid. The drivers use them to lift heavy loads or pump constantly to assist the team from the back of the sled. Some, like Joe Runyan, will run virtually the entire race behind the sled. He attributes a great percentage of his success to his superior physical condition.

"Anything you can do to get yourself in better condition before the race, you should do. It makes you more alert, helps you make better decisions. Every factor helps. If you can run up a hill, that's one less hill your dogs have to carry you up. The big factors are good dogs, good preparation and strategy. But when it comes down to the minutes and seconds, being in shape helps. If you're in shape and you're running against someone who isn't, you have the edge. And they know it."

The sound of dogs waking up and barking to stretch their vocal cords echoes across the river as the dusk of early evening starts to gather. Evening comes early during the northern winter, just as morning comes late. During winter, daylight doesn't arrive until around 10 a.m. and it is already fading when two o'clock in the afternoon rolls around.

As mushers appear on the ice strolling casually from the city to the campground, the barking grows even more intense. It's time to go and the dogs know it.

The order of departure may be different than the order of arrival. The last musher to leave Fairbanks departed from the start line almost 90 minutes behind the first one. That time difference is corrected during the Dawson City lay-over.

For the last musher to leave Fairbanks, his or her stay in Dawson will be exactly 36 hours. For the first driver to leave the starting chute — Gerry Riley this year — the stop will actually be about 37 and a half hours.

It is here, where the race restarts after taking a break, that the musher is again irrevocably separated from the other people now standing in the dog lot. For the moment, he or she is surrounded by officials, handlers, reporters, friends, family, casual spectators and some of the partyers from Diamond Tooth Gerties. They talk

Passing a ship in the day. Dawson City, 1989.

driving with them and laugh with them. But when their time comes, all of the others are left behind. The driver, and the dogs, are the ones who must go back out there.

Monson and Swenson are professional dog mushers. They, like a professional baseball player or professional hockey player, make their living by going back out there. Victory increases the value of their teams, enhances their winning reputation for endorsement purposes and the prize money more than covers the bills. But the Mitchells, Tingeys, Turners, Reiters and Randalls of dog mushing aren't professional. They will lose nothing by not returning to the trail. Just the fact they have made it this far is testimony to their exceptional devotion and talents.

For them, there is only the knowledge that reaching the finish line will be a personal triumph. They may not be this year's champion and will probably not even recover the cost of competing with whatever prize money they may pick up, but they will have done their best, for themselves and their dogs. It is enough. When their time comes, they will drag themselves across the river, load their sled and pull out.

Dave Monson looks rested as he packs his sled. A good sleep does wonders for the confidence a musher feels. Recalling how down he felt about his dogs upon arrival, he has a pretty positive attitude about them now. He will be the first one out but Swenson, who is working around her sled, and Riley, who hasn't turned up yet, will follow close behind.

"I don't think anyone else will be fast enough to keep up to us," he says with a smile, "I expect that Kathy and Gerry will catch me when I stop for a break."

Being the first isn't necessarily an advantage. There are still 400 miles to the finish line in Whitehorse and plenty of time to make mistakes. In fact, it is almost as if there is a hex upon drivers who leave Dawson City first. So far, the first team out of Dawson has never won the Yukon Quest.

Joe Runyan led the way out in 1984, but finished fourth. Rick Atkinson left Dawson with a seemingly insurmountable twelve-hour lead in '85, but ended up second. Sonny Lindner started breaking the trail out in 1986, but was the fourth driver to reach the finish line. Kathy Swenson was first out last year and she also came up short at the end, finishing fourth.

Right on schedule, with the light of the stars and a new moon reflecting off the crystalline surface of the river, Monson pulls his snow hook and "hikes" the dogs. Riley is due up next, but experiences some checkpoint jitters: he oversleeps and arrives just a few moments before his time to go; there are problems packing his sled; his headlamp refuses to work for a while, he misplaces a harness, then a pouch on his sled breaks. Finally, he leaves, 30 minutes behind schedule. Swenson, who has been in the campground for a few hours now, watches and waits patiently, then she too is gone.

Bruce Lee peers into the eerie light of the river and watches as Swenson fades into a spectral shadow, made real by only the narrow beam of her headlamp bobbing along the ice. He has another two hours to wait.

They're going to be tough to catch," he sighs, "It could happen if the weather turns bad or they take a wrong turn or something. However. . . ." Lee knows, as does everyone else that anything can still happen to change the outcome — improbable, but not impossible.

The teams are like pieces on a 1000 mile chessboard. Every time a piece is moved or put into play, the whole game can change.

Footnotes

1 The Klondike Gold Rush left an indelible mark on world history. It was the last of the great gold rushes that opened up the unexplored portions of the earth's surface. It came at a time when there was a depression languishing from the Crash of '93 and the Twentieth Century was looming with no hope for an emotional or commercial lift to relieve the universal feeling of hopelessness. Like a lottery, it gave people the chance to dream of a new future full of previously unimagined and unlimited opportunity. While only a few thousand actually made it to the Klondike and vastly fewer tasted the wealth, the millions who were never there but who felt the magic of that time talked about it for the remainder of their lives.

2 The scar is the result of an ancient landslide which carried down a substantial portion of the mountainside to cover a large part of the moose pasture which eventually became Dawson City. It is part of local Indian lore that a village and its inhabitants was buried by the slide.

OVER THE TOP

It was the squeaking of a dog sled runner on the dry snow that inspired northern journalist Elmer "Stroller" White to write his infamous newspaper story about the Dawson City ice worm plague in the winter of 1900-1901.

The story, printed worldwide, informed the "outside" (the rest of the world outside the Yukon-Alaska area) that extremely low temperatures combined with a heavy fall of blue snow had resulted in thousands of ice worms leaving their burrows in the mountain glaciers surrounding Dawson to bask in the cold.

The problem, continued White's article, was that basking ice worms tend to chirp constantly and the incessant noise was keeping the unfortunate people of Dawson awake at night. Unless warmer temperatures drove them back into their natural habitat, drastic steps would have to be taken to control the beasts.

If an ice worm control program was ever initiated it was never recorded, but the ice worm became an instant part of northern legend. And if there was such a control program, it was apparently to collect them and use them for "Ice Worm Cocktails": a clear alcohol based drink that has a long white worm in the bottom. It is not very appetizing to look at, but in truth, is usually just a piece of spaghetti with eyes painted on it. Such is the substance of legends.

Whether or not the ice worm really exists is a matter of somewhat dubious speculation. The United States Department of Agriculture does have a file on it, but the prime source of information was the author of the newspaper article. Research is hard to get due to the fact that ice worms only come out when blue snow falls and the temperature falls below minus 70. But if the ice worm does exist, it will probably be found on The Dome.

King Solomon's Dome is one of the tallest mountains in the Klondike region and the highest point on the Yukon Quest trail. From its summit radiate the six creeks that were the focal point of the Klondike Gold Rush. Its name was given to it by disgruntled miners who searched its slopes fruitlessly for the mother lode from which

Dawson

Yukon River

Bonanza Creek

N

25 kilometres

King Solomon's Dome 4045 ft.

Indian River

Sulphur Creek

Sulphur

Eureka Dome 4327 ft.

Stewart River

Maisy May

all the placer gold in the creeks must have come. They never located the lode and mockingly named the prominent landmark after the forever lost central African gold mines of King Solomon.

If anything could lure an ice worm from its home, short of blue snow and minus 70 temperatures, it would be the squeak of sled runners on snow as the teams pass over the moonlike landscape above the treeline. An ice worm probably wouldn't come as a surprise as strange things often happen to teams while they're on or around King Solomon's Dome.

Don Glassburn met the ghost of Solomon Dome in 1987. Tired and cold, he stopped to build a fire and feed the dogs. While perking up a pot of coffee, he debated about whether or not he should continue down the trail right away or get some sleep.

A man suddenly appeared out of nowhere and told him it was 35 miles to Dawson; it was worthwhile getting a rest. Glassburn didn't question the man, who wasn't dressed for the cold and simply vanished the same way he came. He settled down to get some sleep.

Another team came by. What are you stopping here for, the driver asked Glassburn, it's only 15 miles to Dawson — so close it was worth a last push for the night. Glassburn got up, hitched up the team and headed out. "The ghost was right. It turned out to be 35 miles."

Frank Turner misses a turn in the dark when his dogs make a sharp right onto a road and he doesn't catch the trail marker. "There's this steep, icy road with some sled marks on it. I thought, 'Well. O.K. This must be the way' and I got up there and we're going by this mine site. There are lights and everything and I thought, 'This doesn't look like the trail to me.' But there were those sled runner tracks in front of me. I kept on going.

I never knew in Dawson, they have an underground mine in the side of a hill. It's up on the Dome. It's this big hole and the whole team started to go down it. I was freaking out because we're on ice and the brake won't dig in properly. And they're freaked out because of this big hole and they just keep heading into it. Finally I get us stopped, turned around and out of there."

Later, no one else on the Quest admits to having knowledge of the mine or its location. Turner never finds out who, if anyone, made the tracks going into the mine.

The trail from Dawson City, after leaving the river, climbs over, then follows along, a series of ridges overlooking the gold-bearing creeks for a short distance until it reaches the foot of the Dome.

Ralph Tingey leaving Dawson City, 1988.

There it connects with a series of switchbacks, trails that cross from one side of the hill to the other along a slightly inclined trail. At each end the U-turn takes the musher a little higher on the hill, then they head across the hill towards the next U-turn. It is slow going up the side of the Dome. The area, from the point where they leave the river to the top of the Dome, is crisscrossed with mining roads and the remains of old cabins.

It appears to the drivers that wherever they can see the highest and steepest hill, that's where they'll find the trail.

Charlie Boulding, originally from North Carolina's Blue Ridge Mountains and now living in Nenana, Alaska, will decide in the 1990 race that he has the perfect explanation for the trail missing the smaller, more easily climbed hills.

"The trailbreakers get lost, and when they get lost, they do the same thing I do when I get lost. They go to the top of the biggest hill and take a look around."

The climb to the summit is considered to be one of the more difficult ascents on the trail. Switchbacks can be extremely wearing on a team: the corners are steep — dogs and musher must work hard to get up and around. Then, looking back along the hillside, they are demoralized by the realization that they travelled that far along the trail and worked that hard to gain only a few feet in elevation.

Looking up, the drivers can see only trees. Occasionally, a gap in the forest gives them a view of the sky and false hope that they've finally reached the top. Then they turn the corner and it's just another switchback that seems to stretch forever across the face of the mountain.

It can grate on even the steeliest of nerves, driving mushers like Jon Rudolph in 1987 to ride up the hill screaming at the top of his lungs, "This is the stupidest thing I've ever done! I want out of here!"

Lena Charlie puts out a supreme effort to conquer the climb and never stops working all the way from the bottom to the top. "I had to push the sled all the time. It was dangerous because the sled was so heavy that when I went up steep slopes it would start to come back down on me."

Falling off the trail can also be a pain. It's hard enough when they pull over on the side of the trail to rest and feed the dogs. They usually pull into soft snow and it takes a terrific effort to get back onto the packed trail. Slipping off the trail on level ground is also cause for extra work. But when they fall off the trail on an incline, the sled usually tips over into the snow on the downhill side. Then they have to unload all the gear, dog food and camping equipment, pack it up above the trail and stack it there, lug the sled uphill back onto the trail, and reload everything.

If one team falls off the trail, it creates a huge hole at the side of the track. Each team that follows usually falls into the hollow, creating an even larger trap for the next team to deal with.

Harry Sutherland and Sonny Lindner were battling their way from one hole to another on the way up the Dome in 1984; they both managed to fall into every one. Right in front of them, Mary Sheilds was doing the same thing.

"We would help Mary out of the hole," Sutherland said, "Then Sonny and I would fall into the hole she made and we would have to dig ourselves out while she went on ahead down the trail."

Finally, Sutherland and Lindner got past Sheilds when she took a break, then they fell into another hole. They dug themselves out, and heard Sheilds coming down the trail behind them.

"Let's get the hell outa here," said Sutherland, and they did before she could arrive.

This is the final mountain barrier on the trail and traversing the summit has the potential of disaster. If the moon had a climate, this is probably what it would be like: barren, lifeless, windy and cold. Like on the Eagle and American Summits, a stiff breeze creates minor problems this year.

Vern Halter, the Alaskan lawyer who will win the Quest in 1990, is tipped over a bank by the wind. Turner, who is close behind, starts down the hill towards him to help. Looking back, he sees a gust of wind rock his sled over onto one runner, threatening to send it and his dogs crashing down on top of Halter's team below.

"Vern, I've got to get out of here," Turner shouts as he retreats to his sled, "This is not a good place to stay."

The Dome has been kind to the mushers most years. In 1984 and '85, it provided them with calm, safe passage. In '86, it burdened them with lots of fresh snow. The strong winds made their appearance in 1987, along with drifting snow and extreme cold.

Bill Cotter smiles when he thinks of the Dome summit that year. In the midst of a blizzard and minus 40 temperatures, he had a birthday party and ended up spending the night with Kathy Swenson.

Cotter, Swenson, Jeff King, François Varigas, Dave Monson and Jon Gleason pulled into the leeward side of a shallow cliff for protection from the storm. Somewhere in the discussion, two facts emerged: nobody wanted to go any further tonight, and Cotter had turned 41 two days earlier.

"We were all stuck there in the storm so we decided, as long as we're stuck, we might as well enjoy it," remembers Monson. "So everybody got out their treats, like barbecued chicken wings or ribs or roast beef or cake or whatever you had and we had a birthday party."

The food was turned over to Swenson who turned it into "something delicious," as Cotter puts it.

"She's a helluva good cook," says Gleason. "I think she gets more pleasure out of cooking than she does driving dogs."

Swenson and Monson had already formed an informal partnership on the trail because of her culinary talents. At one point, Monson had pulled out to pass Swenson who had stopped for a rest.

"It's a trap she laid for me. I was passing her on the trail when I smelled Beef Wellington. My dogs wanted to go on, but my stomach forced me off the trail. We've been travelling together ever since. She cooks and I change the runners."

Even as the six sat around the fire enjoying the birthday dinner, Swenson was eyeballing the sleeping tent that Cotter had rigged on the side of his sled. It was a big, black bivouac bag that used the sled as a tent pole and anchored to the ground. She contemplated the howling winds and swirling snow.

"Do you think there's room for two in that thing?" she asked Cotter.

"Yup," he replied, "There's lots of room."

"Well," suggested Swenson as she gathered up her sleeping bag, "It's the least I can do for a man on his birthday."

The two of them bedded down in their respective sleeping bags, sheltered in Cotter's tent from the wind and insulated from the ground by a caribou mat.

"It was," Cotter says, "one of the most wonderful birthdays I've ever had. And I don't even think anyone sang 'Happy Birthday.' "

By morning, the snow, pierced here and there by breathing holes, was all that could be seen of the camp. It was only when they collided with a couple of buried sleds and woke up a few dogs and drivers that Marc Boiley, Ralph Tingey and John Shandelmeier even realized there was somebody there in the early morning light.

"They were camped right on the top of the mountain, in the middle of the trail, all sprawled out," described Tingey. "We crunched a few thermos bottles when we went by.

"We renamed the Dome, 'Sleeping Bag Hill,' " smiled Shandelmeier.

When it's clear up top, with no wind or snow to obscure the view, a musher can pause and look behind to watch the other teams snaking their way up the side of the mountain. It will be like that in both 1989 and 1990.

Switchbacks don't seem so bad when you're going down them. The descent down the back side of the Dome is almost effortless. The work and the screaming to get to the top of the Dome just about wore Rudolph out in 1987. By the time he had crossed the top and started heading down the back side, he was so worn out he fell asleep on the back of his sled. When he woke up, the dogs were barrelling full speed down the side of the mountain. On one side of the trail the steep bank went straight up and, on the other, it dropped straight down. He grabbed the sled to save himself and dug in the brake to slow the team down.

"If you're trying to kill yourself," he muttered to himself, "You're going about doing it the right way."

Lorrina Mitchell had been in a car crash just a few months before the 1984 Quest and it had left her with some fear of going fast downhill. Travelling with Ron "Old Potato Nose" Aldrich (when his nose freezes it swells up and turns red like a potato) and Senley Yuill that year, she relied on their knowledge of the area to prepare her for the big hill on the back side of the Dome. Every time she reached a descent, she asked Yuill, "Is this the bad one?" and every time he would respond, "No, this one isn't too bad. I don't think we have to rough walk [wrap chains around the runners to slow the sled] yet." When she reached the bottom, she realized he had duped her.

"But it worked, didn't it?" she said, "I really give him credit. Senley has to be one of the coolest cucumbers I ever met."

The end of the switchbacks brings the teams through the ruins of Sulphur (an abandoned gold mining town named after the mineral springs near by) then down Sulphur Creek. At the bottom the drivers rumble over the Indian River flats, then climb up to skirt around the side of Eureka Dome.

If the trail went over the top of Eureka, it would be the highest point on the trail, but it only goes most of the way up before turning down the other side. It then runs through the rolling forested slopes of the Black Hills, along trapping trails and down Black Hills Creek.

The area is still heavily worked by mining dredges and heavy equipment. Roads, old and new, run in every direction and mining camps, some abandoned and others just shut down for the winter months, are scattered throughout. Beyond that is the unofficial checkpoint at Maisy May, on the banks of the Stewart River.

The heavy traffic through the area can often obliterate the trails or wipe out the markers. In 1984, Wilson Sam lost the trail in the Black Hills, then went through some overflow and got soaking wet. Finally, getting totally confused, he found himself in a dead end canyon. He turned his team around and spotted a sign nailed to a tree at the end of the canyon. "Bad Luck Gulch," it read.

"They don't know the half of it," he muttered in reply. A couple of hours later he found a trail marker and continued on his way to Whitehorse.

On this side of the mountain, just a few miles into the longest stretch between checkpoints — 300 miles from Dawson to Carmacks — the driver is truly isolated when it comes to helping the dog team. There are no veterinary facilities and no way to call for help when a dog goes down. It is knowledge, ingenuity, quick action and desperation that means the difference between life and death for the dogs.

Ed Salter and Jeff King were breaking trail in 1987, snowshoeing ahead of their teams. Behind them were the dogs and sleds and right at the back was Rick Atkinson, who was trying to keep all three teams — his own, King's and Salter's — in order.

King's team bunched up, then stretched out again. The tow line got wrapped around one dog's neck, then the dog lost its footing, was dragged and was being gradually strangled by the line. Unaware of the problem behind them, King and Salter continued on. Finally, stopping for a breather, King glanced back over his shoulder.

"What the hell is Rick doing?"

Salter looked back. Behind them, Atkinson had left his spot at the back and was digging frantically in the snow beside King's team. He grabbed one dog that was standing in his way and threw it aside.

"What the hell . . . ?" exclaimed King.

He started back towards the teams just as Atkinson reached into the snow and pulled out another dog, limp and apparently lifeless. He unwrapped the tow line from its neck, then forced the mouth open. Lifting the eyelids he saw the eyes rolled back, showing only the whites. The tongue was discoloured and the animal wasn't breathing.

Atkinson remembered that when he had attended agricultural college in Scotland, he had been told to breathe down an animal's nostrils when giving mouth-to-muzzle resuscitation. Maybe that worked for cows and sheep, Atkinson wasn't sure. He had never had to do it before and he didn't do it properly this time. Instead, he leaned over and blew hard directly into the dog's mouth. He breathed again and again. He looked up at King and said, "I think we lost him." But he gave it one more try.

The eyes of the dog rolled like a couple of pinball machines. It gave a little start, then coughed and started to breathe.

"I didn't walk up to the team thinking I'd do that," said Atkinson," But until I got the dog sorted out, I didn't realize he was out of it. I did what came naturally to help. It's no big deal, it's just luck. Lucky for Jeff really."

There was silence. The three teams stood immobile, the falling snow disturbed only by the weak wagging of the dog's tail. Years of life and death experience in the arctic had not prepared any of them, man nor beast, for what they had just witnessed.

Necessity broke the spell: they had to keep moving or risk becoming further snowbound. King loaded the dog onto his sled and the three drivers resumed breaking their way through the snow. As they continued driving one surprising consideration occurred to Atkinson: that he might actually end up regretting his actions if King and his miracle dog went on to beat him across the finish line.

It was a prophetic thought. King did finish ahead of Atkinson in 1987 and the revived dog was in harness at the end, but the big Scot never regretted it for one moment.

One year later, less dramatic but no less effective, is Dennis Kogl's cure for one of David Sawatzky's lead dogs. The animal simply lays down in the middle of the trail and won't get up. Sawatzky loads it into his sled and it just flops over, eyes cloudy, displaying no interest in food or water.

After carrying the animal for 30 miles, Sawatzky starts to worry. If he has to carry it all the way to Carmacks, it will exhaust the rest of the team. When he comes across Kogl, he asks the veteran for advice.

"This dog had a dump lately?" inquires Kogl.

Nope. Not since getting a pill in Dawson City to stop a brief bout of diarrhea. Kogl runs his hand over the dog's stomach. It is hard as a rock, the intestines are distended. The anti-diarrhea pill has done its job, maybe too well.

"I think I can take care of this," Kogl announces as he turns to his sled and campstove over which he is heating water for dog food.

He pulls a rubber tube out of the sled, cuts off the ends, inserts it into the dog's rectum and pours warm water down it. Pulling out the tube, he drops the dog on the snow where it lays spread-eagled with a perplexed look on its face.

"Will this take long?" asks Sawatzky. Kogl doesn't respond. There is no need to. It doesn't take long. The dog has one bowel movement, crawls a few feet and has another. Then it stands up, gives a shake and looks back at the mushers, its pride dented but not broken. There is no fairy-tale ending for this dog, however. Sawatzky has burned out his team by battling with the leaders through the early stages of the race and scratches in Carmacks two days later.

Many miles ahead of them, Monson is breaking trail by himself. Riley and Swenson tarry a short distance behind him. With any luck, they hope, he will wear himself down. Bruce Lee has fallen well off the pace and now drops to fifth as a charging Rick Atkinson catches up to him.

Maisy May, 1988.

"I may have taken too much out of my team on the way to Dawson. They don't seem to be getting their speed back," explains Lee.

Maisy May is a musher's favorite as a stopping place. Harry Sutherland rates it as one of the high points along the trail.

"I'm reminded of the Bible passage about the widows —'They gave out of their poverty' — because those people live simply and you get some donuts, granola, home-made bread, coffee. That's what they have to offer and that, to them, is probably worth more than 30 steaks to someone else. They're doing the most they can do and I really appreciate the people at Maisy May."

In fact, the Bible analogy is very appropriate. The tenants of the cabins, originally built as a hay farm in 1897, are Mike and Vicki Fletcher, members of a Christian religious commune affiliated with the Living Word Ministry. They have been part of the Yukon Quest since it first appeared in their front yard in 1984.

Race judge Ed Foran and marshal Jon Rudolph arrive by plane, landing on skis on the river ice. Both of them know Maisy May hospitality from having raced the Quest in previous years. "It's a real neat stop," mumbles Foran through a mouthful of coffee and donuts, "It's a welcome break. Everybody's exhausted when they hit Maisy May."

However, 1988 is the swan song for the Fletchers. They will leave the Yukon in late 1988 and in future years their place will be filled by volunteers flown in to run a ham radio base.

The trail, along which Monson leads the Quest into Maisy May, runs across part of the 100 cleared acres of land the Fletchers cultivate in summer. Then it twists around some fences, past a few abandoned buildings, then between the barn and blacksmith shop to arrive at the two-story main cabin.

In daylight, there isn't much problem negotiating the track across the property. But at night it can be confusing since there are several other tracks crossing the marked trail.

"It's quite a big area," smiles Mitchell. "It's quite easy to get turned around and forget where you put your dog team."

Swenson is starting to get impatient. She finally overtakes Riley just five miles from Maisy May, pulls away from him and follows Monson in an hour later. Monson simply smiles when she suggests his dogs look tired from breaking trail.

"We're fine. You just can't get up a lot of speed when you're breaking trail."

Riley breezes in. His dogs' feet look sore, but their tails are up and they appear rested.

"I didn't want to push too hard to get here," he says, "But I did want to make sure I was in a position where Monson can't get a jump on me in Carmacks."

The spot where Swenson passes Riley is just about the same spot that Jon Rudolph and Sutherland passed a gang of teams camped out in 1986.

"How come you guys are camped here," asked Rudolph, "Maisy May's only about five miles further down."

"Oh no," replied Bruce Johnson, "It's still a long way from here."

Sutherland and Rudolph looked at the group as they huddled around a bonfire trying to keep warm in the minus 40 degree temperatures, then at each other. It didn't look like too much fun. Besides there was a warm bed just a few miles down the trail. They kept on going.

It wasn't until the next morning that they heard anything more from the drivers camped with Johnson. Sonny Lindner had been one of the campers and now he stormed into the room where Rudolph and Sutherland were sleeping and started kicking Sutherland's bed.

"Come on you sonofabitch," Lindner snarled, "No way you're going to sleep. We spend the night out at 40 below and you're here. No way you're sleeping. Get up." The other drivers joined in, making so much commotion that sleep was impossible.

Atkinson has become a new factor in the chase for the finish line. He is still five hours behind Monson, but his time from Dawson is the fastest so far.

"My dogs won't have had as much rest as Monson or Swenson when we leave here, but we'll be with them. Especially if there's trail to break. Nothing is impossible as long as the leaders are in sight," he says, noting with satisfaction that the three teams ahead of him are still parked in the yard when he arrives at Maisy May.

Behind them, teams are stretched out for 200 miles. Fourteen teams are somewhere in the mountains and hills between Dawson and Maisy May. Eight are still waiting in Dawson for their departure time. Seven are either on American Summit or running the Yukon River, heading upstream from Eagle.

The number of casualties continues to climb. Adolphus Capot-Blanc's dogs have a flu of some sort and he decides they have had enough. The jovial trapper from northern British Columbia, called the trail jester for his endless sense of humour, will return in 1990 but he won't finish that race either. However, he will gain his place in the history of the race by being of such service to the people along the trail that the mushers will award him the most coveted prize, next to the winner's paycheque: the Sportsmanship Award.

Clifton Cadzow had burned up the trail from Eagle, and burned out his team. His leaders were getting rebellious and balked at following his commands. "I pushed them too hard over American Summit in the heat of the day and now they're not with me. If I go on, I could ruin them forever. At this point they don't trust me any more." He scratches at Dawson City.

Minutes are now becoming crucial and while it's not yet time to reveal their grand strategy for victory, the frontrunners are starting to play games with each other.

The drivers behind the team breaking trail have an opportunity to study the leader. The team directly in front has to concentrate on locating the trail. With no sled runners to follow and markers being knocked over or buried, Monson has worked a little harder than he wanted to. It has worn him down more than he wants.

"The problem was, I was first one on the trail. There's nothing and nobody ahead of me so I had to make sure I was right. It took an awful lot of concentration."

He has to sleep, but while his eyes are shut, he doesn't want Swenson — whom he considers his prime competition at this time — to sneak out of Maisy May and build any kind of a lead. He watches for his moment, then lays down on top of her coat and dozes off. If she has any clandestine plans for leaving, she will wake him up when she pulls her coat out.

But she doesn't pull it out. And he doesn't sleep very well anyway. He can't relax, wondering why she doesn't even try. Maybe her team is stronger than he thinks. Maybe Riley's isn't as slow as pre-race evaluations had indicated.

Riley is really starting to get on his nerves. For a guy who wasn't supposed to be a threat, he is proving damned hard to shake. Atkinson is moving fast too. Too fast maybe, or is he showing what his team is capable of doing?

The eyes are closed. The body apparently at rest. But behind the eyelids, the brain keeps ticking.

The race route is called The Gold Trail because it passes through the site of almost every major gold discovery in the Yukon River watershed. Therefore, it must seem ironic to race organizers that the price of gold has been a thorn in the side of the mushers since the race's inception.

It was pure coincidence: in the early 1980s, the value of gold took off in meteoric style, climbing from $32 per ounce to over $800 before dropping back to settle at about $400. The increased price and demand for gold generated interest in previously mined regions that could still be productive with improved techniques and equipment.

Access to some of the gold fields is through marshy areas that are impassable for heavy equipment in summer. The solution is to travel over those roads in late winter and early spring when the ground is still frozen and capable of supporting the weight. Cat trains — convoys of trucks and trailers pulled or led by bulldozers that push the snow aside to permit passage — have become a common occurrence on back roads and bush trails in late February and early March.

One of their regular routes is along an old road that parallels Scroggie Creek, a short-lived minor gold producing area in 1898. The road is primarily used to gain access to the Black Hills area from the Pelly River, almost 90 miles south of Maisy May.

When the organizers of the Quest laid out their trail in 1984, using the long-abandoned stagecoach road between Dawson City and Whitehorse, the 90-mile road along Scroggie Creek was part of the route. It was about that same time the gold miners decided to use the same area to reach their gold claims.

Neither group knew what the other planned and for the first four years of the race, the two have literally met head-to-head. They will continue to confront each other for the next two years while the Quest organization attempts to find or develop an alternative trail that will avoid the conflict.

Maisy May

Stewart River

Yukon River

Scroggie Creek

Grand Valley Creek

Wounded
Moose
Trail

Pelly River

Pelly
Crossing

Minto

Midway
Lodge

Mt. Freegold Road

Yukon Crossing
(abandoned)

N

25 kilometres

Carmacks

Jon Rudolph is in Maisy May to let the mushers know that the cat trains started to move the day before.

"You may run into a cat train," he says to the lead group of mushers in the cabin. "We don't know when they're moving, and there's nothing we can do about it." There is already ten miles of exposed gravel on the trail that they spotted while flying in.

How long the teams will spend on the cat train road depends on where they are positioned in the race. The front runners run along the plowed road for between four to 15 miles. The campers at the back face travelling up to 70 miles on exposed gravel and rock. Almost all will meet a piece of heavy equipment of one sort or another along the way.

When Jeff King said in 1984, "Anything a stagecoach can get over, my team can get over," he, like the organizers, envisioned a wide, snow-covered throughway cut through the woods. No one had any idea of the chaos of ice, rock and dirt the teams would encounter along the Scroggie Creek road.

Leroy Shank was driving along quite comfortably in '87, pushing through a series of small creeks and ravines, when he came across a Caterpillar parked on a patch of gravel. Passing it, he found himself running along a wide dirt trail. "I realized this is the infamous mining cat-train road. The worst thing was that it wasn't like frozen dirt. It was mud. The dogs were walking in mud up to their knees. Booties were worthless. This stuff was like glue and just pulled them off."

After a few hours of this, he stopped to wait for nightfall. By the time he was ready to go, it was snowing slightly and the air was cooler. The mud had started to freeze up and get hard.

"It helped a little, but it wasn't good going by any means."

The cat blades not only push aside the snow, they also bust up massive boulders into jagged chunks and churn up broken shards of shale. Lorrina Mitchell finds the surface is especially bad this year.

"They'd taken most of the snow off and the musher had to walk an awful lot of that because it would take the weight off the sled and help prevent wearing out your dogs and your runner plastic. I hit some really bad stuff that just got stuck in the runner and opened it up like a razor blade."

Jim Reiter changes five sets of runners and endless numbers of booties when he travels over 70 miles on the mud and rocks. "The further back in the race you were, it got progressively worse. It took an awful lot out of the dogs."

Dogs suffer sprained knees and wrists. One of Kathy Swenson's cuts his foot on a piece of shale and the wound becomes infected before she reaches Carmacks. She is forced to drop the dog at that checkpoint.

Each driver has his or her way of dealing with the cat train trail. The front runners get there as early as possible so they will run over as little of it as possible. The drivers in the middle of the pack have to run over a little more so they try different ways of coping.

Ralph Tingey tilts his sled and rides on one runner to reduce the drag on the dogs and minimize the damage to the runners.

Vince Stack, who ran his first Quest in 1987 with the goal of finishing it without turning into a wreck, just cursed it from one end to the other. It didn't improve the running surface, but it made him feel better.

Most merely resign themselves to the fact that the trail will be better suited for trucks than it is for dogs and they will just have to endure the inconvenience.

Few drivers will ever forget the harrowing experience of encountering the equipment itself.

Mitchell turns a corner and her leaders come muzzle-to-blade with "the biggest piece of equipment I've ever seen. This thing was literally right across the road. It had one side of it's blade stuck into the mountain and the other end hanging off the road and there was no way around it. I made sure they saw me before they ran over my dog team." She squeezes past when the cat skinner (bulldozer driver) is able to pull off to one side a few yards further down the road.

Hans Oettli, a heavy equipment mechanic from Switzerland, experienced a little déjà vu in '87 when his team encountered the cats. The last time he had been on this particular stretch of road, he had been operating a piece of equipment at least as large as the one he now faced. There was no place for the cat skinner to move off the road so he turned the cat slightly, swinging the blade out from the side of the hill and opening a passage for the dogs.

Oettli drove his team into the gap and stopped in the narrow area between the cat treads and the mountain. The dogs were intimidated by the heat, noise and size of the machine.

"My dogs had never seen a piece of equipment like that. You usually don't see that on a trail in wintertime. They went in with one command. They looked a little nervous. I'm sure they didn't like it." The cat skinner then swung the blade back into the hill behind the team and moved the back end out to open an exit for them. "I operate cats once in a while. I know how much precision you have in turning a track. I just hoped he was a good operator."

The verbal exchanges between the drivers and the heavy equipment operators range from friendly and sympathetic to unfortunate harshness. The cat skinners are the victims of the drivers' frustration even though their presence on the road is the result of decisions beyond their control (mining company executives decide when to start moving along the road). Most of them insist they try to accommodate the mushers as much as possible and minimize their effect on the race while, at the same time, trying to do their job.

The Yukon mushers who are in the construction and heavy equipment business know several of the drivers personally. Jon Rudolph jumped up on the running board of one truck in 1987 and stuck his head in the window.

"Jon," exclaimed the startled driver, "What the hell you doing out here?"

"I'm in the Yukon Quest."

"God I didn't know you were in the race. Sonofabitch, we haven't seen any other dog teams. You must be in the lead!"

"Yeh, I know that. But not for long. The rest of them are just back a couple of miles. They'll be coming along pretty quick. Say, could you guys pull over for a while so we can get by?"

"Sure. No problem."

Looking back on that day a couple of years later, Rudolph concludes that despite everything, "They were really pleasant to deal with, and they went out of their way to try and make things as easy as possible for us."

Jim Reiter has a slightly different view of the cat skinners and truck drivers. He knows what he wanted to tell them as he struggles over the miles of shale and muck, but he can't find any of them.

"By the time we got through, the operators made themselves real scarce. I imagine after about the fourth or fifth guy gave his opinion about how they were doing on the trail, they didn't want to talk to us anymore. We saw a lot of equipment parked along the road, but we didn't see anyone around it."

Parked equipment was a blessing for Shank in '87. Wet and tired he came upon a truck parked on the side of the road. He stopped the team, gave some snacks to the dogs, then tried the door of the truck. It was open.

He crawled inside. There he fired up his stove, hung his wet gloves on the sun visor and parka over the back of the seat and cooked up a Cajun meal of red beans and rice. Dry, rested and fed, he climbed out and continued on his way.

"I looked for a registration. I thought, well I'm going to thank this guy, whoever he is. But I never found one."

Dragging the sled over the road is one of the more frustrating hardships the drivers encounter in their thousand miles, but it wasn't the cat trains or their legacy that forced a group of six drivers out of the 1987 race in this area. It was snow: far too much snow.

A storm rolled in behind the front pack of mushers, dumping over four feet of snow into the Scroggie Creek area in 24 hours. The leaders just caught the leading edge of the storm. Those behind them had to battle blustering winds and swirling snow at the outer reaches of it. But right in the middle of the storm were the six teams bringing up the rear.

These trailing teams had all fallen behind for various reasons: Jim Reiter and Craig Wolter just had slow teams; Kelly Wages had broken through the ice earlier; Larry Grout, a former professional downhill ski racer and rodeo bull rider with a fast team, had been delayed when he stopped to help Wages; Ty Duggar's sled had needed constant repair and Hans Oettli's team had been fighting a dog flu for the past 200 miles.

When the drivers started that morning, the sun was shining and the trail hard-packed and fast up to where the gravel started. Three hours later, Oettli couldn't see his lead dog, 40 feet ahead of him, because of the snow. The cat-train road, cut down to the bare earth with three foot embankments on either side, was barely discernible as the snow quickly filled it. Trees, overburdened with snow, leaned over like drunks then snapped off and fell across the trail.

Duggar and Oettli took three hours to travel three miles before stopping to rest. Grout, Reiter and Wolter caught up to them and then pushed past, but only for a few hundred yards. They stopped and debated the situation.

There wasn't enough food to get to the next checkpoint if this storm covered the rest of the trail. A food drop (additional food flown in by airplane) along the way would automatically disqualify them. It was suggested that the food from all be concentrated on two sleds, which would continue ahead while the others turned back.

In the end, it was decided that they would all turn back and return to Stepping Stone (a popular stopping point for the mushers

Stepping Stone, 1989.

located on the Pelly River). On the way down, they met Wages and he joined the retreat.

In hindsight, agree the drivers , they made the right decision. They had no way of determining how extensive the storm was or how far they would have had to travel to get clear of the snow. In fact, it was over 100 miles before their next opportunity to get off the trail and every inch of the way was buried under the snow. It would have been impossible to make it with their limited supply of food.

But the decision to stop racing — to scratch — is one that the driver finds difficult to justify, no matter how right it may be. "A lot of those things go through your head," says Reiter, "There is a lot at stake in this. You probably had a lot of support from friends, the community, sponsors and stuff. . . did I wimp out and take the easy way out when the going got tough or should I have kept going? Did we quit too soon? We just didn't know, that was the thing.

I honestly believe that anybody who starts this race doesn't think they can't finish. That's simply the furthest thing from your mind. The only question really is, in what position will you finish? It's ingrained in your mind — there's no problem finishing. Then . . . I was completely taken aback when all of a sudden I couldn't go anywhere any more."

Even a year later, Oettli still has doubts. "It's kind of hard to explain that afterwards, you know. I'll never really get over the idea that I should have kept trying. I always think there should be a way. Some people just have bad luck, I guess."

The reasons a musher has for scratching vary from individual to individual, but the most common cause seems to be an overwhelming concern for their dogs.

Bob English broke into tears and cried when scratching in Dawson City after contemplating the toll the trail was taking on his dogs in 1984. Jon Gleason endured frozen fingers, a frostbitten face and exhaustion to the point of losing control in '87, but when he discovered his dog Dutch had frozen his foot he withdrew immediately, just 100 miles from the finish line.

While the cat-train road is getting longer for the lingerers, the road to the finish line is getting shorter for the leaders. Swenson is riding hard on Monson's heels as he rides into the yard at Stepping Stone, just seven miles down the Wounded Moose Trail from the end of the cat-train road.

Race judge Ed Foran, watching them roll in, is impressed with the quick time they have made since leaving Dawson. "It looks like, when they're not camped, they must be going 10 miles per hour, which is really fast for this stage of the race."

There are beds at Stepping Stone, but this is not the place to be caught napping. In previous years, owners Lou and Carol Johnson had set up cabins for the mushers to sleep in. But as the race matured and became more competitive, fewer of the drivers took advantage of the sleeping facilities. Yet, at other times, the opportunity to use the cabins at Stepping Stone can be used strategically. It's a guessing game to try and figure out who is in which cabin and how long they plan to stay.

"By the third race, they didn't want to tell anyone how long they were going to stay," smiles Lou Johnson, "It got very confusing sometimes. Trying to sort out who's where, what cabins are being used and trying to keep it all secret."

None of the drivers want to lose track of their competition by this stage in the race and, rather than use the cabins, they sleep on the kitchen floor or in the workshop so nobody can sneak away undetected. It gets a little crowded at times, with a dozen or so drivers sprawled out over the floor.

Stepping Stone is a place where races can be won or lost. It is here where, for some reason, otherwise race-wise drivers make major mistakes. François Varigas, in '87, picked this stretch of trail to try and blow the race wide open.

The tall, bearded Frenchman opened up the throttle and arrived in Stepping Stone a good hour ahead of his competition. He stopped for an hour, then kept on driving. But it was premature and two days later Varigas conceded defeat as he lay inside a cabin while outside his team refused to move any further without more rest. "They're depressed," he said, "And so am I." They did eventually finish.

Harry Sutherland lured Sonny Lindner out of a warm cabin at Stepping Stone into a cold campsite on the Pelly River in '86. Sutherland stopped long enough to peer in the window at the coffee and donuts piled on the table, then considered the minus 40 temperatures and drifting snow.

"I knew that every one of the sonofabitches coming behind me is going to stop here. I looked and going out there was a freshly broken trail. I just looked around and said 'let's go.' I don't think they even knew I was there."

The broken trail only lasted for a mile or so before dead-ending into waist-deep snow. When Lindner arrived at Stepping Stone, he only stopped for a few minutes. The fact that Sutherland hadn't stopped bothered him. He took off from Stepping Stone and found Sutherland camped at the end of the broken trail. He got bogged down in the snow also. The two of them spent an uncomfortable night in the cold night air, while behind them the other drivers snoozed happily on the warm kitchen floor.

By morning, those who had stayed at Stepping Stone had caught up to the two drivers. Their gamble had failed to pay off. The trail they thought would give them a big lead had fooled them and the night spent in the cold took its toll. If either one of them had asked Lou Johnson, he would have told them the trail was only a mile until it hit deep snow. It was a mistake that contributed to keeping them out of the winner's circle that year.

This year, the trail is unencumbered by the heavy snows of the previous two races. Past Stepping Stone and across the Pelly River it continues to follow the old stagecoach road which was built in 1902 between Whitehorse and Dawson. The stages rolled over this extremely hilly route until the Klondike Highway between the two cities was completed in the late 1950s. It's near Minto Flats where the teams leave the stagecoach road and move over to run alongside the Klondike Highway.

174   YUKON CHALLENGE

The trail doesn't actually go into Minto Flats, which used to be home to an Indian Village and a wood camp for the riverboats. But passing close should give even the most exhausted team an extra reason for trotting past this spot as fast as possible.

Minto is the multiple murder capital of the Yukon. The first was a sensational triple killing at a place called Hootchekoo Bluff, just a few miles from Minto in the winter of 1898-99. The last occurred in the early 1960s: an apparent triple murder-suicide that was never really resolved since no cause of death was ever determined for two of the victims. Six months later, the woman who discovered the bodies was herself shot to death. Shortly after, the final inhabitants of Minto packed up and moved out.

All that remains at Minto now are a few derelict cabins and an emergency air strip. There are some permanent residents further down the river, mostly trappers.

The trail bypasses Minto Flats, then turns out to run alongside the Klondike Highway to a gas station called Midway Lodge, about ten miles from Minto. It is the first place where handlers and family can see their driver and team since the teams left Dawson two days earlier.

When Monson pulls into Midway Lodge in the early morning hours of the race's tenth day, he is 300 miles ahead of Ty Halvorson and John Ballard, the final two teams that are still on the Yukon River heading to Dawson. Between them are spread 34 more teams, of which only three apparently have a realistic shot at Monson's spot.

Although Monson stops and grabs an apparently casual coffee and donut, his eyes keep glancing nervously down the trail. Somewhere back there in the trees and poor light are Riley and Swenson. They may be running without lights — creeping closer without being seen — or camping just around the corner, out of sight, hoping he believes they are further behind than they really are.

"My feet are really sore," he complains to a couple of bystanders. His nerves finally get the better of him and he pulls out after only 10 minutes. Riley appears just 20 minutes later and trots past without stopping. He passed Swenson sometime during the night, but she is just five minutes behind. She doesn't stop either.

Rick Atkinson is still within technical striking distance, but when he reaches Midway it is obvious that he doesn't have a realistic chance. While the front three are moving steadily forward, Atkinson's team is gradually losing speed. They look tired as they trot into

Midway with their tails down and flop gratefully onto the snow when he stops.

Bruce Lee, still in Stepping Stone and now too far behind to mount a threat at this late stage in the race, finds himself being pressured to maintain his top five placing by a pack of teams, led by Kate Persons and John Schandelmeier, slowly but surely making up ground. Dennis Kogl, Ralph Tingey and Jim Wardlow are close behind.

But the pieces are still in play and anything can still happen among the front three. Whatever traps nature doesn't set with snow or storm or encounters with wildlife (Vern Halter will be chased by a moose just out of Midway Lodge in 1990), can be set and sprung by man.

Harry Sutherland found that out the hard way in 1986. Running down the side of the highway towards Minto he could see a road sign on the side of the road, telling him it was only two kilometers to the station. But he was tired and bored.

"You can only watch dogs run for so long." As is his habit on long, straight pieces of trail, he turned his back on the team and sat on his little seat, facing back down the trail.

"Suddenly the world went dark. Stars flew. Then I opened my eyes. I was lying face down in the snow and the team was heading on down the trail. I thought someone had hit me with a two-by-four. I lay there wondering, 'Who in hell would hit me here . . . Why?' "

Then he looked directly above him and saw the road sign. And it dawned on him that the trail didn't take a little loop to go around it as he assumed it would; it went directly under it. And it wasn't tall enough to get under without ducking behind the driving bow.

Even with the finish line within sight, figuratively speaking, the drivers are by this time starting to get convinced that this trail is going to go on forever and there's no checkpoint at the other end, just more trail: a sort of eternal punishment in dog musher's hell. But even the road to hell has detours.

With their bodies and minds sapped by ten days of driving and deprivation, it gets easier to become confused and get lost — even when you're not lost.

Sonny Lindner was out front by himself in '84 when he stopped to camp. He was hoping to be able to time the next driver to follow. But, after six hours, nobody had turned up. Concerned that maybe he was on the wrong trail, he started back up the trail looking for markers. After a couple of hours he found Harry Sutherland.

"Is this the trail?" asked Lindner.

"I don't know," replied Sutherland, "I'm following your tracks." Lindner smiles when he's reminded of that time. "I wasn't lost," he says, "I was misplaced. It was the right trail all the time. I just didn't think that anyone had let me get six hours ahead. You get a little confused in the middle of the night."

Ed Salter couldn't seem to locate anything in 1987 — no trail markers, no tracks, nothing. After awhile, he became convinced he was on the wrong trail.

"I finally stopped and said, 'Well, if I'm going to be lost, I'm going to be lost stopped.' It was the right trail but you're half fried, haven't slept, you can't see a marker even if you're looking right at one and you don't know if you're on the right trail or not."

The race is no longer measured in distance. Now, it is easier for the driver to gauge performance by time. They know what time they left the last checkpoint and they know what schedule they're running to rest and feed the dogs. But it's impossible now to determine how fast the dogs are travelling.

"I don't know," Jeff King will answer in 1989 about how far it is from Maisy May to Dawson City, "I left there at 6:30 last night."

From Midway, the trail returns briefly to the Yukon River, then crosses a long hill strewn with loose "widow-maker" boulders[1] on a slope "so steep you need to take a run at it to get up," says Oettli. It then drops onto the Freegold Mine Road (an access road to several small mines in the hills south of Carmacks) for the final 20 miles into the checkpoint.

Monson's feet are still the first thing on his mind as he pulls into Carmacks.

"My feet are killing me. All I want to do is get out of these boots," he says, glancing at his watch. He has to stop here for a mandatory six-hour veterinarian inspection before continuing. He can't afford to leave one second later than he is allowed to and he has to watch for the next two teams, to determine just how big a lead he has when he leaves. Even though the race takes almost two weeks to complete, there is not much room for error this close to the end.

The biggest margin of victory in the last three years has been 24 minutes: Bruce Johnson's triumph over Jeff King in 1986. In '85, Joe Runyan reached the line just 20 minutes ahead of Rick Atkinson. Last year, it was Monson himself who was nipped at the wire by Bill Cotter. The difference between the paycheques for first and second

Jeff King, Vern Halter and Jim Wilson keeping close, 1989.

is $5,000. Monson can attach a dollar figure to each 60-second segment: $500 per minute — that's what his ten minutes cost him last year.

Alone in the dog lot, Monson seems only concerned with one thing: feeding his dogs. Then his focus seems to come slightly unravelled and a startled nervousness flashes across his face as Riley rolls up a half hour later. It is supposed to be Swenson.

"I'm right where I wanted to be," says Riley. His persistent ability to catch Monson is obviously starting to have some effect on the younger driver.

Last year, Monson had been duped into dismissing Cotter as a threat, then didn't have the speed to overcome his lead at the end. That another master strategist can steal a second one away from Monson is looming as a definite possibility. Riley must be faster and stronger than everyone gave him credit for when this race started. But how much faster?

Swenson pulls up an hour later. Her team looks strong and confident, loping in across the line with their tails up. She parks her dogs then glances at Riley before walking over to Monson.

178

"He's chasing you, Big Time," she indicates Riley with a nod of her head. Monson gives her a tight smile.

Later, looking across the yard at the two drivers, she laughs, "David's going to be driving with his neck backward tonight, I think. He'll have a sore neck when he gets to Whitehorse." She makes no mention of herself being in the chase. She looks good; her dogs look good.

The tight finishes that marked all three of the last races prompt former Yukon Quest International president Dick Underwood to observe, "The only thing I'm betting on is that a lead dog will be first across the line. But I won't bet which one."

Footnotes

1 Widow-makers are large rocks that lie loose on the sides of hills. They can be easily dislodged, go crashing down the hillside and kill someone.

STUMP COUNTRY

In 1984, Carl Huntington stood silently in a small huddle of different opinions in the recreation centre gymnasium in Carmacks. Last year, Leo Oleson sat alone at a table in the checkpoint in Dawson City, rubbing the exhaustion from his eyes. Tonight, Jon Rudolph hunches over against the night's cold on the road outside Crabb's Corner in Central. They are all individuals poised on the brink of making a decision that may or may not affect the final outcome of the race; a decision that everyone will hate or a decision that only half will hate.

In every race, there must be one person who is the ultimate authority: who can mediate disputes; who can be the judge, jury and both lawyers when investigating protests; who can take abuse and can hand it out and can enforce the rules or change their interpretation when needed and apply common sense to situations that make no sense. When Carl Huntington took on the job in 1984, he stood up at the pre-race mushers meeting and faced the mushers. "I'm the race marshal," he said, "What I say goes. Any questions?" It was not an invitation to ask any.

Huntington's meeting with the race judges and race managers in the gymnasium of the Carmacks Recreational Centre demanded a resolution he knew would affect the final outcome of the race. The trail from Carmacks to Whitehorse ran alongside or right on the Klondike Highway for the first 40 miles or so. He had to sort out all the options: find an alternate route., run it as it stands or bypass the dangerous section. Everyone had a different idea. But it was on Huntington's shoulders that the final decision and ultimate responsibility lay.

"You can't run a dog team at night on or beside the highway with a tractor trailer coming down. The dogs will be blinded and turn right out into the middle of the road," he explained when announcing his decision.

Carmacks

Little Salmon River

Yukon River

Mandanna
Lake

Chain
Lakes

Frank
Lake

Frank
Creek

Coghlan
Lake

Klondike Hwy.

Nordenskiöld River

1985
Trail
Braeburn

1984
Trail

End of
trucking 1984

Fox
Lake

Lake
Laberge

Fox Creek

Richthofen
Island

25 kilometres

He had spent several hours scouring the hills, seeking an alternate route that could be prepared quickly. There wasn't one. The teams would be loaded into trucks and driven past the dangerous section to Fox Lake, 50 miles from Carmacks and 75 from the finish line in Whitehorse.

Some drivers complained that the shortening of the final leg was a detrimental factor in their final positionings, while others lauded it for its safety aspect.

In 1987, another difficult decision had to be made. When an airplane pilot reported there were four teams on the wrong trail coming into Dawson, Leo Oleson just wanted to get away from the confusion of the checkpoint and sit by himself for a moment. He was tired and hungry and he knew what was coming. The four mushers had missed the marker at a turn-off on one of the ridges. They would blow into town on a plowed and broken pathway while behind them, the rest of the teams busted their way through the fresh windblown snow on the actual trail.

The protests made for a long sleepless night as Oleson and race judge Jon Rudolph pondered over what would be a suitable penalty. In the end, the four drivers were given a six-hour penalty, extending their mandatory stay in Dawson from 36 to 42 hours.

"Getting lost is part of the race," explained Rudolph, "But gaining a direct advantage by taking the wrong trail isn't allowed. There's a fine line there. Some people wanted them heavily punished. Some felt that, since it wasn't intentional, it should be light. We had to find a compromise so we assessed them six hours. There was still a lot of bitter feelings, and no one was happy so we sort of figured we must have made the right decision because everyone was mad at us."

"We didn't call it a penalty because it wasn't," says Oleson, "It was an attempt to put everybody back on an equal basis." One of the four penalized drivers, Bill Cotter, went on to win the 1987 race.

Tonight, Rudolph fills the role of race marshal. He stands on the road in Central and faces a hoard of angry mushers in the cold. Two teams had taken the wrong trail for a few miles, saying they knew it was the wrong one but that they couldn't find the right one. Other drivers suggest they opted for the road rather than breaking trail and gained a definite advantage because of it. As the protests continue, he makes two decisions. The first one irks the mushers.

"Look," he says to them, "Some of you guys also missed part of the trail out there. And it's too damn early in the race to be screwing around with this kind of stuff. Just get on the goddamn trail and keep racing."

The second one prompts phone calls from the organizers and rules committee in Fairbanks.

"I made the decision to break a trail, to make sure there was a definite trail. Most of the infractions and major hassles occur because of trail conditions or markers. I was in that 1986 race when Bruce Johnson won it, and the trail conditions were the shits. We broke trail for 600 miles."

The order to have snow machines re-break the trail all the way to Whitehorse raises a few eyebrows in Fairbanks. For the purists, it is contrary to the philosophy of the race. The mushers must be self-sufficient: if there isn't any trail, that is part of the wilderness experience and that's what they have to cope with.

"What the hell are you doing Jon, sending snow machines out to break trail," demands the voice on the other end of the telephone, "That's not the intent of the race."

"Well," he replies, "If you put dog drivers in here as race officials, I guarantee you there's going to be a broken trail all the way to Whitehorse. If you don't like it, get a new race marshal."

"No. No. That's fine. Do whatever you're going to do."

So he does. The trail is broken for the rest of the way. In the end Rudolph's insistence on sending out the snow machines finds favour with the majority of the mushers and the majority of the organizers. He will be invited back as race marshal for the 1989 and 1990 races.

Not all the problems are so monumental or the resolutions so controversial. The marshal and the two race judges spend most of their time monitoring the teams on the trail, checking the tags to be sure the drivers aren't switching in fresh dogs and ensuring the mandatory gear is in each sled at each checkpoint. They are the official back-up for the veterinarians in enforcing dog-care rules and watch to see if mushers receiving any kind of outside assistance are actually gaining any advantage because of it.

Penalties can range from disqualification to a time penalty where a musher isn't permitted to leave a checkpoint for a specified period of time. One driver was penalized two hours in 1985 for outside assistance when he pulled dogs' chains out of his truck and used them. Another will be given the same handicap in 1989 for leaving Dawson before the end of his 36 hour layover. "If a trapper helps out a guy or gives him a place to stay, he must do that for every musher," explained 1985 race judge Sam Johnston.

Bill Cotter talks with vet Carl Monetti, 1984.

Officials are constantly bombarded with stories of violations, most of which are the products of vivid imaginations.

"It's like a soap opera," says Rudolph, "Everyone's coming up, trying to dig up dirt, trying to get something going. The media's probably the worst for it, but the handlers are just as bad. The mushers aren't too bad, they're just out there racing.

But you got the handler sitting there, they've got nothing to do, so they start making up stories: this guy's cheating or whatever. You sort of have to block all that out. If you start listening to it, you just get sidetracked. You've got to go with only formal complaints, a good eyewitness, or catch the guy yourself."

Just like the drivers, there's not much time to sleep for the race officials or the veterinarians. Not only do they have to keep track of the leaders, but they can't lose touch with the campers 300 miles behind or any of the teams in between. And mushers don't exactly run on bankers' hours. They run when they feel like it, when their team will go or when the weather permits it. No matter what time of day or night, the officials and vets have to be there.

A lot of their time is spent crammed into small aircraft flying back and forth between the checkpoints. Huntington, Oleson, Roger Williams and Leroy Shank had to pile into a small Cessna in Dawson in

'84. Williams went up front beside pilot Les Bradley; Shank and Huntington crawled into the seats behind.

"He [The pilot, Les] looked at Leo [Oleson]," remembers Williams, "And he just kind of pointed. Leo looked. 'You want me to lay down in the fuselage?' Bradley said, 'yep. 'So we all loaded up and Leo crawled back in the fuselage. All of a sudden the nose of the plane went up and the tail went 'thunk.' I look over at Les. 'Do you really know what the hell you're doing here?' He said, 'Don't worry. It'll straighten up just as soon as I get the prop going.' He fired it up, the nose came down and before I could think about it, we were in the air." It wasn't until 1985 that Oleson, in his first year as race marshal, was able to see the trail between Carmacks and Dawson from the air.

They ride in cars and trucks when they can, usually in the Circle District where so much of the trail is close to a road, or on snowmobiles, especially from the Yukon River checkpoints.

The snowmobiles put them on the same playing field as the drivers and they must cope with the same dangers. Williams and trailbreaker John Mitchell jumped on snowmobiles in Dawson City in 1986 and headed up the trail to see what damage had been done by a wind storm the previous night.

As Williams stepped off his machine to reset a marker about 20 miles from Dawson, the snowmobile cracked through the ice, then was slowly sucked into the black water. He looked over at Mitchell who had just stepped off his machine a few yards away and watched dumbfounded as the same thing happened to his snowmobile.

"We broke the first rule: we didn't tell anyone where we were going." The two built a fire and layered on clothes that Williams carried in a rucksack on his back. For almost 48 hours they tended the flames, kept warm and waited for a rescuer to happen by. Finally a trapper did come by and he carried them to Dawson.

At any given moment during the race and in any likely or unlikely location, the veterinarians can be found pinching the back of a dog's neck to test for dehydration, inspecting paws and leg joints for cracks or swelling, drawing blood or trying to coax a dog to urinate in a jar so they can screen it for drugs. The urine is collected in a small styrofoam cup hooked onto the end of a rod. They usually wait until after the dogs have been fed and watered before selecting an animal at random to be tested. There aren't any fire hydrants in the wilderness, so the dogs are led past trees, bushes, piles of snow —

Tom Randall (R) and vet Sue Cullen taking a look, 1988.

anything that may inspire them. When the animal gets the urge, the vet sticks the cup underneath and fills it. It's then sealed and shipped to a laboratory in Vancouver, B.C.

Steroids and blood-doping aren't their prime concerns. Drugs that can suppress symptoms of illness or mask injuries, such as common aspirin or anti-inflammatories, are their main targets. Finding traces of any banned drugs results in automatic disqualification. So far, everyone has tested clean.

The vets wield the power to order the musher to drop a dog or completely disqualify the team if, in their opinion, the dogs aren't healthy enough.

Lolly Medley, a veteran of the Iditarod, was forced to withdraw in '86 after she had gotten lost near King Solomon's Dome and travelled an extra 50 miles in deep snow. The extra work burned out her team and caused serious foot problems. Upon arrival the vets ruled that four of her dogs weren't capable of continuing, one over the drop limit that year.

Mike Maurer, a fisherman from Salcha, Alaska, will be disqualified in 1990 after one of his dogs dies shortly after arriving in Carmacks. The injuries suffered by the dog will lead the vets to believe the animal was not given proper care on the trail. Maurer will protest the ruling, insisting that the autopsy gave the vets a false reading, but his disqualification will stand.

Usually, however, the musher already knows when a dog has been hurt or when a team has been burned and will reach the decision to drop the animal or scratch entirely before a vet even sees the dogs. Checking at each official checkpoint and turning up often at the unofficial ones is a safeguard to guarantee the dogs are getting the best of care.

Dennis Jackson will be the vet on call in Dawson City in 1989 when the Quest arrives. On his first Quest, he will quickly learn respect for the musher's relationship with the dogs.

"One musher told me, 'It's like having 12 children.' "

"This is a race where the mushers have to take care of their dogs because there is a dog drop limit and 1,000 miles is a long way to go," says four-time vet and one-time racer Karen Schmidt of Anchorage. The commitment of the veterinarians is so strong that they will fly from just about anywhere in the United States and Canada to work without pay for two weeks in the bush. There are usually 10 of them spaced out along the trail each year.

Jim Reiter has good reason to appreciate the extra effort put forward by the vets. When one of his dogs chewed off its foot after freezing it at Stepping Stone in '87, Terry Quesnel, a vet from Vernon, British Columbia, flew in, landing on the snow-covered ice of the Pelly River, to perform a quick bit of surgery that saved the dog's life.

The dogs take all the pinching, poking of needles and peeing in jars in good humour. "The sled dogs I've seen back home are vicious," smiles New Jersey vet Jean Buist, "Here, the greatest danger I've had near a team is being licked to death."

The six-hour mandatory lay-over in Carmacks, a small hamlet that serves as a convenience stop on the Klondike Highway, is a veterinary stop. It is the final opportunity to give the teams a proper check-up before they head off into the home stretch.

Dave Monson doesn't spend an idle moment in Carmacks. His stove blazes constantly as he feeds the team, then cooks up meals for further down the trail. Meals prepared in advance mean he can cut unnecessary time off any snack breaks, and he can leave the stove behind. He strips down the non-essential gear, reducing the weight of the sled substantially. There will be no stopping after this unless it is absolutely necessary, and with only 150 miles to go, sleep can wait until the finish line.

The contrast between his intensity and the relaxed, confident Riley is sharp. Riley seems content: he is moving casually, but still managing to accomplish a fair amount of work without seeming to. He had used subterfuge and sheer toughness to become an Iditarod champion a decade earlier and now seems to be flexing those same qualities.

"The dogs and I talked it over and tried to decide what we want the other mushers to do for us," he cracks."Breaking trail seems to be what we hope they'll end up doing."

His history of mind games reminds everyone that they should be leery of anything he says. In '84, he constantly mentioned to Jack Hayden that one of Jack's dogs looked sick despite the fact that it was pulling well. Eventually the conviction in Riley's voice convinced the less experienced driver that the dog was sick—although in fact it was perfectly healthy — and he dropped it.

Monson keeps narrowing his concentration. He focuses in on what he must do to win. "I was hoping that somebody else wouldn't have my mindset and say, like I was saying, 'I don't care what the lead is. I'm going to go for it anyway.' "

As the two leaders silently prepare for departure Kathy Swenson is across the dog lot, apparently still in the race. She is doing all the right things: lightening the load, cooking extra meals. But there is something missing. There's no air of anticipation, no tension.

Monson is obviously uptight. He can barely restrain himself. Riley seems casual, but his darting eyes and restless dogs betray that he too is struggling to keep his emotions under wraps. Swenson is methodical, stepping through a routine she knows well, but there is no competitive edge. Even her references to the race hint at capitulation.

"I don't have much reason to hurry now," she says, "I plan to turn on my radio to listen to the finish. And Atkinson will have to sprout wings to catch up to me."

Atkinson, still in fourth, has slipped even further back. He won't even arrive in Carmacks until shortly before Swenson is due to leave.

Monson slips off his boots and puts on his snow joggers (insulated running shoes). He rarely stops glancing at his watch, then, precisely on the second, he slips the snow hook and pushes off into the darkness.

Riley allows his departure time to slip past, taking his time to pack things the way he wants them before finally pushing off a half-hour late.

Sonny Lindner on trail at north end of Fox Lake, 1984.

Swenson leaves on time, 40 minutes later, just as Atkinson makes his appearance in the dog lot to start his six hour lay-over.

The trail drops back onto the Yukon River for a short distance heading east, then turns south along Mandanna Creek, along the length of Mandanna Lake, then through a series of rolling hills before dropping into the Chain Lakes. Beyond that, it runs through a small group of hills, then onto Frank Lake and Coghlan Lake and, finally, along a series of small creeks that take them to lower Lake LaBerge, just 40 miles from Whitehorse.

In 1984, the trail bypassed all of the Chain Lakes area and ran along Fox Creek because of the trucking of the teams from Carmacks to Fox Lake. "A suicidal, really wild little piece of real estate," according to Lorrina Mitchell. It was a narrow path through a heavily wooded area, that kept winding along trying to spear the drivers and dogs on dead trees that stuck out from the sides.

In 1985, after following the Klondike Highway for a while, the trail struck out cross country from Braeburn Lodge to Coghlan Lake then turned south[1]. It was a clean, fast trail. Only Joe May had any real problems and that was because he lost his glasses. He mushed along, almost blind, until he noticed a sign on a tree. He kept peering at it, but was unable to read it, so he edged a little closer. It probably said something like "Danger. Steep Hill." But May never really had a chance to find out. His team and sled took off down the hill, with the driver virtually flapping in the breeze behind, hanging on for dear life. The dogs reached the bottom safely and continued trotting down the trail while May thanked heaven he couldn't see what had just happened. If he had been able to see, he probably would have tried to control it and ended up in a pile at the bottom of the hill.

It wasn't until 1986 that the trail was put through where it is today. That year the snowfall was so great that trailbreaker Tracy Harris, who lives in a cabin at Coghlan Lake, could only manage to travel eight miles before turning around and breaking the same trail back the same eight miles through even deeper snow. The coarse snow crystals wore the hair off the dogs' legs up to their knees, bogged down the sleds, tripped up the drivers and turned what should have been a final sprint into an endurance test.

But 1987 was undoubtedly the worst of the lot, giving this stretch a fearsome reputation. Not much snow fell in the months preceding the race; the stumps of cut trees stuck up through the meagre cover and felled trees, usually under the snow, lay on top of it. The trail twisted and turned back in on itself, much like The Enchanted Forest near Circle City had been in 1986.

Jon Gleason remembers his dogs missing a turn in the trail in 1987. He stopped the team and walked up to turn his leaders around, but just a few feet ahead of his team he saw the trail come back down and straighten out again. The turn he missed was just a very sharp loop. He led the dogs forward through the bush and skipped the loop completely.

Mitchell passed through the Chain Lakes at night that year. To help herself negotiate, she put fluorescent tape on her dog harnesses. "When the tape disappeared suddenly I slowed up, because I knew the team had rounded a sharp corner."

"I couldn't go five feet without barging into a tree," said Bill Cotter, "It was unbelievable. I got tipped over, banged into trees, thought I was going to get killed. I thought the sled was going to self-destruct and I'd just let all the dogs loose and walk home."

"If I closed my eyes to envision the worst trail I could," shuddered Ed Salter, "I'd never imagine anything as bad as that one was."

It was like a war zone. All along the trail, mushers were getting jammed between trees or found themselves high centered on stumps sticking three feet in the air.

The dogs seemed to form their own opinion of the trail. Don Donaldson, a security guard from Delta Junction, Alaska, finally pushed out onto a lake after missing a few turns in the bush. "My wheel dog, Dusty, looked at me like 'If you don't know how to drive this thing, come down here and I'll do it.' "

"There were places where prayers were more useful than a brake," said Mitchell, as she remembers that the ice along the creeks was just as bad as the trees. She was crossing one patch of ice when she left the sled to assist the dogs. Suddenly she heard a loud crash behind her and the dogs came to a dead halt. Turning, she found the sled had vanished.

Shell ice is formed when the water freezes high in the fall, then drops and refreezes at a lower level. On a river, the weight of the ice would collapse the upper crust onto the lower one. But on a creek, the top shell isn't that heavy and simply stays intact until added weight, like Mitchell's sled, causes it to cave in. Mitchell was fortunate. Her sled, although in a hole, was dry.

Kelly Wages and Larry Grout weren't so lucky. The water of Frank Creek was so crystal clear, the pebbles on the bottom could be counted through a small hole in the ice. It only seemed a couple of inches deep. As the drivers passed during the day a little more ice was broken loose around the edge and the hole got bigger.

By the time Wages came through in the evening dusk, the hole was substantially larger. His sled skidded sideways towards the hole, then caught on something and flipped upside down into the water with Wages under it.

"I panicked. I admit that," he said.

The water was about five feet deep and the stream had a fairly strong current. Wages unwrapped himself from the sled then threw himself back to the surface and out of the water. The dogs were tangled and confused but none had been dragged into the water.

"They strained to pull it forward but even when I pushed from behind, we couldn't pull the sled out. It was too heavy. Everything was soaked."

It was also cold, about minus 30, and everything he needed to survive was in the sled. He stripped naked, climbed back into the water and started unloading the sled. Some bags drifted away, only to get caught on the ice and a small log jam in the opening.

Larry Grout pulled up behind the hole. Not without hesitation, he also stripped down and jumped in to help. For five hours, the two wrestled with the current, the gear, the sled and the cold. When everything was out of the water, they both pawed through their gear in search of dry clothes. A plastic garbage bag had kept one pair of clothes dry.

Mud and water had penetrated everything else and now it was starting to turn into ice. There didn't seem to be any point in starting a fire to dry out since all the wet gear was frozen solid anyway. Wages loaded lumps of clothes into his sled and both drivers headed off again. It was only 70 miles to the checkpoint at Carmacks and getting wet just didn't seem like a real good reason to stop yet.

"Thoughts about quitting did cross my mind, but I figured nothing up ahead could be worse than what I went through back there." Wages and Grout eventually were forced out of the race at Stepping Stone by heavy snows.

The trail in 1988 is a vast improvement. It has been widened and the stumps and deadfall have been cleared out. There are even campsites set up: lean-tos with spruce bough beds, stumps to sit on and split firewood. Swenson can't believe her eyes.

"I'd go through these camps and . . . shoot . . . look at that! If I see one more of those, that's it, I'm stopping. Sure enough I come up on one. I knew nobody was right behind me so I stopped right in the middle of the trail." She stays for three hours.

Dave Monson decides this isn't the time nor the place for a stop despite the appeal of the campsites. He can feel the team as it methodically paces through the trees, and he can feel Gerald Riley breathing down his neck. He has eyes for only one thing: the trail ahead. Even his sore feet are forgotten for the moment.

"The perfect racing moment was between Carmacks and Coghlan Lake when the dogs were up on step. They were going. They were giving me everything I wanted. The trail was beautiful; the terrain was spectacular. It was a full moon, and I was pumped up, and the adrenaline was flowing. I wasn't going to let Gerry catch me. I wasn't going to make any mistakes. I wasn't going to lose the trail. I was pumping for eight or 10 hours until I got to Lake LaBerge."

"Everything in that race is balance," says Frank Turner, "a balance between rest and stress. The only time the balance comes uncorked is right at the end, then you just let everything out. That's when you really start bearing down, physically and emotionally. You've got to be able to maintain, efficiently, the dogs in front of you and do it over extended periods of time when you're really tired. There's no more tomorrows. That's the thing that's hard to learn;

that's exactly what we mean when we talk about driving dogs."

As Monson's team trots onto the ice of Lake LaBerge only 40 miles from the finish line, he starts to look back over his shoulder. Somewhere back there is Gerald Riley. How far back, Monson doesn't know. He only knows that every other time he had counted Riley out or thought he wouldn't ever catch up again, he'd turn around and find the old veteran right on his tail.

Monson knows he has run the best race he could possibly have run. But is it good enough? Above him, the man in the moon has a better view. He probably knows, but he isn't going to say a thing.

Footnotes

1 Braeburn Lodge, a small lodge on the Klondike Highway halfway between Carmacks and Whitehorse, is famous for the large size of its cinnamon buns.

THE ABSENCE OF REGRET

In 1984, Lorrina Mitchell was within a mile or so of becoming the first woman to complete the Yukon Quest when she almost became its first fatality.

There was an open lead in the middle of the river and the trail crossed above it on a sidehill. At the top of the sidehill, her sled lost its grip and plunged down towards the water. Mitchell jumped off to try to control it, but her feet slipped and down she went towards the river. It could have swept her under the ice, leaving behind a mystery as to what had happened. But as she stepped from the sled, she had grabbed the gee rope (a rope used by the musher to help the dogs turn the sled) and when she slipped, she hung on desperately. Swinging down below the sled, she came up short of landing in the water.

The dogs had actually crossed the ice and had a grip in the snow. They strained hard against the tug line, gradually gaining the upper hand. With shouted encouragement from Mitchell who was dangling helplessly against the icy slope, they pulled the heavy load past the point of danger. Their driver pulled herself up the gee rope, hand over hand, until she was no longer in danger of slipping back, then she just lay in the snow for a long minute catching her breath.

"That really got the adrenalin going. I was mad. I thought it would be really disgusting to drown within sight of Whitehorse after surviving all the other ridiculous stuff I'd been through."

Mary Sheilds is only four miles from Whitehorse when her team simply quits. They just stop running and lay down in the snow. Nothing she does is going to get them started again until they are good and ready to get going. She spends several hours on the ice, less than an hour's drive from the finish line, fuming in frustration as other teams trot slowly past her. Even Frank Turner's dogs, who are mostly female and have been the object of amorous advances from Sheilds's mostly male squad for most of the past two or three days, fail to raise more than an interested eyebrow as they go by.

These are lessons that, even with the finish line within sight, nothing on the trail is certain, that the race doesn't end for each individual driver until their lead dog pokes his nose across the finish line.

For those who are driving for the prize money, there are few moments of certainty. They contend with the environment, the emotional and physical state of themselves and their dogs and their own strategy. They must also be aware of where their opponents are, what they are capable of and try to anticipate their thinking.

Physical toughness will keep a team in the hunt, but mental intensity is what will put a team in front. In dog mushing, as in everything else, knowledge is power.

There are two basic strategies in long distance sled dog racing, but there are countless twists and variations in each one. The first game plan is when a group of mushers travel together as a pack, establishing themselves as the leaders. Usually this group will be a mixture of drivers who have to struggle constantly to keep up, some who can keep up yet really don't have the dogs to win and the true contenders.

The faster teams hold back, letting the struggling drivers and slower teams share in the emotional and physical burden of breaking trail. Then, when they believe the time is right, they pull out all the stops and sprint, leaving the others behind.

It is a conservative strategy, designed to give the faster teams control of the race by keeping themselves rested while staying in touch with the front runners. It reduces the chances that a sudden twist in the weather, like the snow storm near Stepping Stone in '87, or a change in the trail, such as the trucking of the teams at Carmacks in '84, could give a slower team the chance to pull off an upset.

Joe Runyan was a couple of hours behind leader Sonny Lindner when he reached Carmacks in 1984. He still believed he had a chance at top spot, but the trucking ended it. Over 120 miles he figured he could catch Lindner and beat him, but over 75 miles, he knew he wouldn't have the opportunity.

"One thing I learned from that was that developments can change the race. If you're going to be racing, you've got to be right at the front."

The second basic strategy is one that requires endurance, speed and a lot of luck. It is a gamble from start to finish which often results in record fast times, but seldom pays off for the gambler.

The objective is to open a commanding lead early in the race, then try to hold it. If the trail is perfect and the team can endure the constant charge, it could work. Dogs that can force that kind of pace for the complete distance may be able to beat a team that is slightly slower over a distance, but has unbeatable speed in a closing sprint.

Nature must also play a part in this strategy. If a storm blows in behind the pace-setter and ahead of the rest of the drivers, the lead could increase while the drivers behind are delayed by having to bust their way through the snow and winds. There are too many "ifs" and "maybes" in this strategy to be popular with the top drivers.

Both strategies have one thing in common: the timing of the break to establish a lead is crucial. Every advantage that can be used must be inserted into the driver's plan. There is a point in both strategies where co-operation is mutually advantageous, but near the end is another point where each driver must run strictly as an individual.

In 1984, all the teams initially travelled as a group, but the stronger teams gradually established themselves in a small front group that pulled a short distance ahead. Lorrina Mitchell, running in the second grouping of sleds, decided to push herself hard between Eagle and Dawson City. She moved along one night at a fairly fast clip, gradually opening a gap between her team and the others she had been travelling with.

Suddenly she saw a fire on the ice ahead of her. Being in dire need of a rest, she took a moment to realize it was the lead group of teams camped just off the trail. She turned off her headlamp and drove along in the dark.

"I just motored past without stopping. I'm sure it got them real nervous, this team just appearing out of the night and blowing past."

Mitchell had vaulted into first place in one fell swoop. But it was short-lived. She stopped to sleep just past the camp and when she awoke, the leaders had packed up and gone past again. She never saw them again until the end of the race.

Sonny Lindner says through his perpetual shy smile that he knew he would win when he looked at Joe Runyan's dogs in Dawson City. They were thinner than his and, in his mind, that was the edge he was seeking.

"You take two teams that can travel at the same speed, but one has to stop to feed more often than the other. That team can never make up the lost time."

He made his move shortly after leaving Dawson City, breaking away in the Black Hills. It was the right call at the right time. Runyan faded; Harry Sutherland and Bill Cotter kept pace, but they had been three hours behind heading out of Dawson and couldn't make up the ground.

Lindner claims he doesn't think about strategy either before or after the start, but there is never any doubt that he is in every race to win.

"I do the things that I enjoy. I like going fast. If that means I'm first at the finish line, that's great. When you're near the end and you know you're close, you give a little extra."

Because the race reverses direction each year, there are two ways for the drivers to approach the final stretch. In fact, the Yukon Quest is really two races in one.

Running from Whitehorse to Fairbanks in odd numbered years, the length of the early legs is draining on the teams. The fastest part of the race is at the end where the trails are more used (more like dog sled highways) and the distances between checkpoints is shorter.

From Fairbanks to Whitehorse in even numbered years, the teams start to tire later in the race as the distances between checkpoints gradually gets longer. The condition of the trails in the latter stages is less reliable simply because they're not extensively used.

It's more of a gamble to press for an early lead while racing to Whitehorse. If the trail's there, the pace-setter can win. If it isn't, they lose. The best strategy in that direction is to be close to the lead, then as fast as you can in the final 50 miles.

There's more certainty of trails near the end being in top notch shape while running towards Fairbanks. Most strategies for this race will be geared towards making a move much earlier than the final 50 miles, usually in the Circle District or on Eagle Summit. But making a break too early can be fatal.

Joe Runyan tried to make his break early in 1984, pushing hard out of Eagle and going without a break to Dawson. He gambled that a 36-hour break would be enough for his team to recover totally.

He was wrong.

"I found out that's not true. Thirty-six hours is not enough. Taking chances and breaking your rest-run schedule often gives results that aren't repairable. You can't make a mistake."

In 1985, he remembered his lesson and didn't panic as Rick Atkinson bolted out of Carmacks and rolled into Dawson City with a twelve hour lead.

"My strategy was: don't pay attention to anyone else. Run the schedule you think makes sense. Establish what your boundaries are. What your dogs can do. The only thing that's relevant is your own dog team."

Runyan maintained his schedule. Run, rest. Run, rest. All he could do was hope that Atkinson's team couldn't keep up the torrid pace that the Scot had run to Dawson City. He realized it was working when he saw a headlamp bobbing along the river in front of himself near Eagle. The only driver in front of him was a tired Atkinson who had tried to bluff the gambler in Runyan, but didn't hold a winning hand of cards.

When he reached Circle Hot Springs, Runyan felt he was in control.

"Atkinson's dogs had lost a little zip and he was going to have a tough time bringing them back." The driver that concerned him most at this point — Sutherland — was a couple of hours behind but "Harry is the master of this end-of-the-race stuff. He's written the book on it."

At Chena Hot Springs, Runyan, who aided his dogs by running behind the sled most of the time, made his final move. It was time to depart from his rest-run schedule — to pull out all the stops. The pay-off was a record time to Fairbanks that will endure into the next decade. He will employ the same strategy to win the 1989 Iditarod.

Lady Luck and a snowstorm that buried the trail for 600 miles overshadowed any pre-race strategy that the drivers would have had in '86.

Sonny Lindner had wanted to break away at Carmacks, but trail conditions were horrendous and anyone trying to shake pursuit that early would simply put his team into a slow cooker. Cotter, Sutherland, Tim Osmar and Bruce Johnson shared some of the trailbreaking duties with Lindner all the way to Lake Laberge through more than a foot of freshly fallen snow. When they crawled onto the ice and stopped to camp, Lindner's team, considered by all the drivers to be the strongest and fastest on the trail, was completely burned. He had carried the bulk of the work. The freshest was Johnson, who had lingered at the back and had only broken trail when everyone else refused to do so.

A short distance ahead they could see a broken trail, the first one since crossing Eagle Summit.

"We agreed that we were all going to water our dogs then, after two hours, we were going to pull the pin and go for it. We were all going to race in," said Sutherland.

But Johnson didn't stay. He pulled out after only 20 minutes and headed down the lake. Then, down the trail the five had just exhausted themselves breaking, came a snow machine towing a large toboggan. It was a government employee who had been working in the bush and had simply followed what looked like a decent trail to the lake without realizing he was on the Quest trail.

"He's making a trail. He's coming down this thing that just took us four hours to go eight miles on. So here comes Jeff King and he goes by us. He did the eight miles in two hours. Even if that's slow, it's still twice as fast as we did it," Sutherland described.

"Osmar took off. Sonny decided to peel out. I took off. Cotter came behind me. We couldn't be more than five miles apart at that point. But we could never catch up again because we let him go for an hour before we took off."

Johnson held the lead in what he later named "The Lake Laberge Charge." King kept closing but ran out of trail, finishing just 24 minutes behind Johnson.

"All we did was wear out our dogs," lamented Cotter, "Especially out of Carmacks. We believed there was a broken trail, but there wasn't. If there had been a trail, it would have been a different winner that year. That time it was a disadvantage to be at the front that close to the finish line."

But all gave due credit to Johnson. While a faster trail may have produced a different winner, his team was the best in the conditions in which they raced and his strategy was the one that worked.

Ironically, Johnson's winning effort was the slowest of the three races he ran — his previous two finishes had been almost two full days faster. It was the longest of the Quests, taking more than two weeks to complete, and is considered one of the toughest races ever run.

Cotter kept re-running the first three Quests through his head for the next 12 months, trying to determine ways to cut time and where was the optimum point to make a break. He thought he had it all figured out, but all that planning almost got wasted when he was penalized six hours in Dawson for taking the wrong trail.

"It was demoralizing. I knew how much I had lost by in previous years."

But by Eagle, he had caught up to the leaders again. There he took the time to reconsider his strategy. He vetoed trying to make a break on the Yukon River before reaching Circle City.

"Other people who tried this strategy always did it too early."

He decided to wait until he was in the Circle District, but also knew he would have to have a distinct advantage before he reached Angel Creek.

The 1987 race was possibly the most strategically demanding of all of the Yukon Quests. There were four teams — Cotter, Monson, Swenson and King — all relatively equal in strength. They all were looking for any weakness that may provide insight into the others' plans or physical conditions: seeing how the dogs held their weight in the cold; counting the booties that each team used — looking for signs of tender feet; trying to interpret the run-rest schedules, to see if they could estimate how long and how far a team would run once it left a campsite; the fast leader hidden in the team dogs that could be pulled out and thrown up front at the crucial moment — a strong, rested sprint leader can add a mile an hour to a team's speed.

"Sometimes they'll pack their sleds, tie it all down and pretend they're ready to leave," says Cotter. "Then they'll find some reason to delay, hoping that someone else will panic, cut their rest time short and head out too fast. It's serious, but at the same time it's fun."

The weather played a major role in Cotter's strategy, although it was not meant to be a factor. It was cold, too cold.

"I was so cold, I couldn't warm up. I could only build a fire and cook for my dogs." He decided that he would only feed his dogs at checkpoints where there was pre-heated water for the team and prepared food for himself.

The cold also aggravated a back injury he had suffered in January and he developed a limp. The pain was draining his energy and when he pulled off the Yukon River into Circle City, it was emotionally the lowest point for him in the race. He was sore, cold, tired and disoriented.

"I know that after the race some people said I faked it. I may have played it up later on but at that time I didn't know what I was going to do next. I was so cold I didn't know if I could go on."

But when Jeff King loaded his sled, Cotter was right behind, limping all the way to Circle Hot Springs. He looked so worn, it seemed like just a matter of time before he would pull out of the race altogether. His back was obviously causing him a lot of discomfort. Monson, King and Swenson had to make a quick evaluation and they decided he wasn't a factor any more. Inside his shell of pain, Cotter smiled.

The back was sore all right, but it didn't hurt as much as it did in Circle nor was it as bad as he made it look in the Hot Springs. Two warm checkpoints had taken the chill out of his bones and while he was still tired, his adrenalin had started to flow. He went to Central and stopped for one last big feed.

As he sat in the corner of the restaurant, King, Swenson and Monson arrived. They had eyes for only each other and spent a long time manoeuvering into sleeping positions where they could keep track of the other two.

"So I said, 'This is it. This is my chance to go. I win the race right now or I don't.' "

He strolled out, apparently to feed his dogs. As the three other lead mushers dozed fitfully and monitored each others activities, Cotter kept on going, climbing onto Eagle Summit on a rare storm-free night. It took about four hours before the mushers realized that no one had seen Cotter for awhile.

"When I got to the top and looked down that long valley and didn't see another team. I knew I had it," Cotter said. When he reached Angel Creek, he had a three hour edge on Monson and King.

"I figured I could just cruise into the finish line." So he ran leisurely towards Fairbanks, oblivious to the fact that Monson was making one last charge.

A few miles from Fairbanks an aircraft circled over Cotter, then headed further down the river.

"I knew it would circle again over the next team, so I watched. When I saw it circle again just a mile or so behind me I thought, 'Oh shit, I'd better get serious.' "

He reached the line 10 minutes ahead of Monson. As he threw his arms in the air and passed under the banner the pain in his back vanished for the moment and he was more awake than he had been in days.

Jeff King will run a text-book race in 1989. He'll travel most of the way with the established front pack, Vern Halter, Bruce Lee, Kate Persons, Sonny Lindner and rookie Jim Wilson (a commercial fisherman in his first long distance race).

In Angel Creek, King will be the third driver to start out on the home stretch to Fairbanks, behind Wilson and Halter. Knowing he has run a perfect race so far, King will let it all out. "I started the dogs into overdrive, and they bolted by and the other teams weren't able to catch me."

Wilson, who will finish third, was flabbergasted at the speed King's dogs had so close to the end. "He left me in the dust. His dogs went by like their tails were on fire."

Vern Halter will watch King vanish down the trail ahead of him in 1989, but he knows he is only a dog or two and a year's experience from having the same kind of finish. The team that Vern Halter will lead to the start line in 1990 is possibly the single strongest squad of dogs to have ever run the Yukon Quest. The power of the team will be demonstrated when he waits an extra five hours in Dawson City for the second musher, Kate ersons, to leave ahead of him so he won't have to break trail. Giving up his five hour lead so easily is a mistake, the other drivers will say, but by the time he reaches Midway, only Jeff King will be close enough to be a threat.

"They were almost connected," King will say of the team that plays catch-us-if-you-can with him over the last leg from Carmacks, and which he will not be able to catch, "They had a spirit about them, the whole team, that was almost supernatural." Halter and his dogs will be the first team to complete the Fairbanks-to-Whitehorse race in less than 12 days.

206

"Winning," says Dave Monson, "Is the absence of regret." In '87, he had two things to regret. Not having reached the finish line ten minutes earlier was one of them. He had underestimated Cotter: the award-winning acting performance had duped him completely.

"In Central, we sat around like a couple of weasels watching each other in a woodpile while the fox stole the golden egg."

The second regret came when he allowed his anxiety to overrule his caution. In his hurry to make up lost ground, he didn't notice an area of weak ice that had broken when Swenson went over it just ahead of him. Dogs, sled and driver all plunged through into Birch Creek. Working the team out of the hole and drying off by rolling in the snow, he pushed on until he ran into Swenson.

"I said, 'Kathy, I just fell in the river there and I'm soaked.' My gloves were like seal flippers. Kathy monkeyed around, tried to chip the ice off the gloves and zippers. We stopped for over an hour which, at that point in the race is ridiculous. But my decision was to take the best care of my dogs and myself."

Then he missed the turn into Angel Creek and spent some time backtracking to find it again.

Monson remembers the ten minutes he has had to regret for the past year. But as he balances on his runners of his sled in '88, looking back at the north end of Lake Laberge, he knows he has made no mistakes he will regret.

"I just stood backwards and concentrated on that one spot in the woods where the trail ended. I watched for 15 minutes, a half hour, an hour, an hour and a half. Finally I couldn't see that spot any more, after two hours, and I knew that Gerry or no one else had entered the lake. That's when I knew I was way ahead. It would take something super human to catch me at that point. And, so, at that point, the race ended."

Riley is almost nine hours behind by this time. While Monson enjoys the feel of a fast, effortless sprint for the past 100 miles, Riley's young dogs have finally run out of steam. They have been catching up to Monson for 11 days and they just can't do it one more time.

Now, resting at Tracey Harris's cabin, an unofficial checkpoint on Coghlan Lake, he is in danger of being caught by Swenson. But she is unaware of his problems and doesn't realize that second place is within her grasp. At one point she comes within a few hundred yards of him, but her team has also 'hit the wall' (run out of steam).

Team crossing Lake Laberge, 1987.

"I was bummed out because I had a chance to catch Riley and I blew it. My dogs were gaining on him until we lost the trail. We went around in circles for about 30 minutes before we found it again." But the extra stress drains her team. They stroll the rest of the way to Whitehorse.

For the drivers, as they approach the north end of the lake, the last few miles become the hardest part of the trail.

The ice that forms over Lake Laberge has a natural beauty to it. A layer of ice seems to be the perfect surface for the long, narrow lake walled on each side by high cliffs. When the sun rises or sets in winter, it turns the ice a light, glowing pink.

The Indians thought it was so awesome that when they described it to Mike LeBarge, a surveyor with the Western Union Telegraph Expedition in 1866, it was in such terms that he envisioned a lake of beauty beyond belief. Although he never saw the body of water that was to later bear his name, he described it constantly and in great detail to others for the rest of his life.

The sun's light gradually creeps down the hills on the west side, and touches upon the rocky marge of the lake — where Robert Service chose to cremate Sam McGee in one of his most famous

208

works — and upon Richthofen Island, where a group of cabins used to provide service and shelter to the riverboats that plied the length of the Yukon from Whitehorse to Nome. Many of those riverboats, having been caught in the sudden windstorms the lake is notorious for, now lie wrecked upon the shore.

But the history and the poetic setting aren't enough to give the tired driver more than a momentary thrill. The bruised and aching of abused muscles can no longer be overpowered by a rush of adrenalin. Once the emotional race is over, there is nothing left except to complete the physical part. Time starts to feel like an anchor: the hours spent alone on the lake ice are the longest ones the drivers will ever endure. It's only 40 miles to the finish line, but the dogs are moving unbearably slow. At times it seems like they're not moving at all. Every second becomes a minute; every minute, an hour.

"I must have fallen asleep twenty times on the lake," Vern Halter will say in 1990.

Dave Monson, a wounded warrior waiting to do battle with an opponent who never showed, feels lonely and sore as he drives the length of the pink ice into the rising sun.

SLEEPING DOGS

The finish line is the last half-inch of space that the mushers must travel in the Yukon Quest. But that final inch is what has kept the drivers on the trail. Without it, everything that came before — 1000 miles of trails and tribulations — is incomplete.

For almost two weeks the drivers have lived an intense lifestyle patterned exclusively around their racing timetables, their dogs' needs and the environment and geography. They and their dogs have run, rested and eaten in eight hour shifts, three shifts a day — all aimed at one ultimate goal, to pass under and beyond the finish line banner. Then suddenly, in the space of that one second it takes to complete the race, it's technically over.

Pressure becomes relief. Solitude changes to crowds. Wilderness trail turns into city streets.

Whitehorse.

Nobody's exactly sure where its name comes from. One story says that an Indian Chief called White Horse drowned in the rapids up river from the townsite. Another, more universally accepted, suggests that prospectors in the late nineteenth century compared the waves in the rapids to the manes of white horses. Whatever the origin, the area was commonly known as the White Horse by 1887.

Whitehorse is the exception to the historical rule on the Yukon Quest. It is the only area that had no gold discovery of its own to bring in the first residents. It served as a sort of checkpoint on the trail to the Klondike gold fields.

While the city of over 21,000 is known primarily as the hub of transportation in the territory, for the dog drivers this year, it is the end of the trail.

Their first clue that the end is nigh is an old abandoned garbage dump on a high bluff about three miles out of town. People often drive out to it, then clamber down to river level to watch the teams go by. Next, the drivers see a power line stretched across the river. Around the next bend and there are cabins in the distance on the far bank of the river; another corner and they can see the shacks in the old shipyard.

212   YUKON CHALLENGE

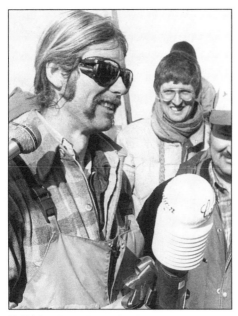

First Yukon Quest Champion Sonny Lindner, 1984.

There is one more little manmade trap to dodge. The trail passes under a footbridge leading from the shore to a mid-river island where one of the support cables under the bridge hangs low enough to decapitate the unwary musher. At night, the cable is wrapped in reflective aluminum foil and a car is parked with its headlights shining on it. So far, everyone has ducked under it.

Then the mushers follow a boat launching road that leads up from the ice to the railroad. The sleds travel alongside the tracks for a hundred yards or so to the parking lot beside the famous White Pass and Yukon Railway's two-storey log train station.

The finish line itself is somewhat unimpressive: a small motor-home parked to one side, two powerpoles with the banner stretched between them, some wooden road barricades to hold back the spectators and three or four sets of portable bleachers so those in the back can see over those at the front.

Inside the motorhome can be found volunteers like Peter Garside and Doug Baird — non-mushers who take holidays or leave-without-pay from work to satisfy their own fascination with dog mushing. They have been race officials for sled dog races in the Yukon since the early 1970s. Along with finish line organizer

Joe Runyan, Quest Champion, 1985.

Dolores Smith and Quest archivist and soon-to-be-mother Edna Knight, they sleep, eat and wait patiently in shifts, 24 hours a day, watching the river for approaching teams. They move into the vehicle a day or so before the first musher arrives and won't leave the area unmanned until the last one is safely across the line. It can be minutes, hours or even days between teams.

Because of the uncertainty of predicting exact times of arrival, crowds at the finish line tend to be small. A few minutes after each musher crosses the finish line, the crowd size almost doubles as news of a new arrival is spread. Those who wait at the line between arrivals are dedicated musher supporters.

When a musher does roll in, the crowds see some unusual things.

Sonny Lindner was the first musher to ever complete the Yukon Quest. When confronted by the media, he shifted uncomfortably from foot to foot, gave shy one-word answers to the questions, then walked past the 166 ounce Texas Mickey of rye whiskey that awaited him as the victor and went shopping instead.

"One good reason for not winning," he will confide a few years later, "Is that you have to talk to the press and give a speech at the banquet."

214   YUKON CHALLENGE

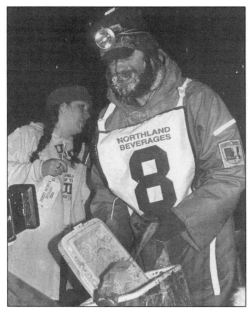

Bruce Johnson, 1986 Champion.

In 1986, Joe May finished his 12-year racing career, that included a win in the 1980 Iditarod, with a camp fire in the finishing chute. Gently, solemnly, a small tear freezing on his eyelash, he officially confirmed his retirement by placing his snowshoes on top of the fire and watching them be consumed by the flame. He is one of the few who retired and didn't come back — yet.

Ron Aldrich is probably the only musher ever to be greeted in the finish area by a woman (his wife) standing in the snow wearing a yellow polka dot bikini. It was minus 20 degrees when Aldrich finished in 1984 and his wife wore a warm overcoat that she opened to flash her garb at him at the appropriate moment. A lot of the bystanders never knew who she was or what she wore, if anything. All they could see were her bare legs under a long coat.

Lorrina Mitchell was the first woman to ride to the finish line in that first Quest in 1984. Only a few spectators were on hand to greet her, but the one she remembers best was sitting across the river from the finish line.

"It was a cat and, you know, the dogs didn't even look at it. They could care less. They could see the finish line across the river. This cat was sitting on the riverbank just terrified, staring at us, but we went right on by."

Bill Cotter winning the 1987 Quest.

The big money was gone, but there was still a little cash to be had when Frank Turner and Wilson Sam trundled into Whitehorse in 1984. They had travelled together for 600 miles. Now, 100 yards short of the finish line, they stopped, drew a line in the snow and sipped on a beer supplied by a bystander. The next one across the line would be 14th, which would earn $100 more than 15th — the last position that earned a cash prize.

The two lined up abreast. The bystander counted down to zero and the race was on: it was Turner by a nose.

William Kleedehn, finishing in 1990, will have found answers to the two questions he started with: he has a long way to go to be able to compete with the Alaskan mushers and his artificial leg isn't a handicap, in fact it's almost an advantage — he only has to worry about frostbite on one foot instead of two.

Jennine Cathers will make her mark in history by finishing the 1989 Quest as its youngest ever competitor. And she'll be back in 1990 for another shot at it—she aspires to be the first woman to win.

Now, in 1988, there are perhaps three or four hundred people waiting to greet Monson as he motors in to claim the championship purse and belt buckle (a custom scrimshawed piece of mastodon ivory).

Dave Monson, 1988 Champion.

"When I realized the finish line was there and I was going to cross it, I didn't even have time to really emotionally prepare myself for the fact that I was going to win the Yukon Quest," he says, "I'd gone from absolute solitude to total pandemonium." A set of headphones slapped on his head connected him with his wife, Susan Butcher, in Anchorage preparing to defend her Iditarod title.

"I hear in my ear ... Susan is talking to me. She's not even there and it's like, 'What kind of a dream am I having?' "

Gerald Riley, who plods across the finish line about nine hours behind Dave Monson, finishes what may well have been his last realistic shot at the winner's circle. He'll be back for another effort in 1989, but the big high-tech kennels, like Monson, Runyan, Swenson and King will keep getting stronger and faster and the old school of dog mushing will realize its day is done.

Kathy Swenson, who in 1987 had been the first woman to finish in the top ten, trails in a couple of hours later to take third place.

Between the championship contender and the one who will light up the red lantern — the traditional prize for the final finisher of a dog sled race — come the rest of the pack.

Rick Atkinson.

Bruce Lee, who finally gets a last minute burst of power from his dogs to hang onto a top five finish.

Kate Persons, who many believe will actually become the first woman to win the Quest. She will be back in 1989 and 1990, both times — like Kathy Swenson — coming close.

John Schandelmeier. Dennis Kogl. Ralph Tingey.

Jim Wardlow. Vern Halter. Frank Turner. Lorrina Mitchell.

Mary Sheilds. Her uncooperative dogs, now rested, perky and happy, finally got up off the ice and brought her the rest of the way to Whitehorse.

Ron Rosser. Ned Cathers.

Cathers trots in a few hours ahead of Lena Charley. He's tired, but he had fun. "I'm only going through life once and I have no intention of not enjoying himself." The outdoor adventure guide will return in 1989 and 1990.

Lena Charley pulls up after 15 days on the trail. The quiet, durable grandmother was 20th in 1986 and she's 20th again this year.

Jim Reiter. Tom Randall.

The red lantern finally goes to Ty Halvorson. He out-delays John Ballard to wander casually across the line a full week after Monson finishes.

He joins the ranks of other notable slow-pokes - Shirley Liss in '84. She had to actually finish in Carmacks because the ice on the Yukon River was too rotten to travel on when she reached it. Jim Bridges in '85. Michael Schwandt in '86 and Allen Dennis in '87. Peter Butteri in 1989 and Esa Eckdahl in 1990 will also collect their own red lantern.

Behind them, left behind in checkpoints along the way are Jon Gleason, David Sawatzky and his constipated dog, Don Donaldson, Clifton Cadzow, Bob Bright and his futuristic sled, Adolphus Capot-Blanc, Jeff King and Francois Varigas. All are out for this year, but most will return in 1989 and 1990.

In all, 30 of the 47 mushers, who pulled out of the starting chute in Fairbanks two weeks ago, will reach Whitehorse.

And when they arrive, each one wants to do something different.

Jon Gleason just wanted to go dancing in '85. As a past president of the Alaska Trapper's Association he wanted to arrive in time for the annual Trapper's Fling Ball. He rolled into Fairbanks at six in the evening, and the ball was scheduled to start at eight. After a shower and a meal, Mary Gleason wanted to get her husband home.

Jeff King, finally a Champion, 1989.

"No," he argued, "We've got to go to the fling."

He sleepwalked into the ball, yawned at a few friends, then turned around and headed to bed without dancing a single step.

It will be in the 40-foot chute beyond the finish line that Will Forsberg will finally catch his wife, Linda, in 1990. She will be ahead of him all the way from Fairbanks, leaving taunting notes at each checkpoint to goad him on his way along the trail. By the time he arrives, she will have had a shower and a sleep before coming back out to greet him.

This year, sitting in the checkpoint when Halvorson rolls in is Jeff Fisher. Tired and dirty after three weeks on the trail, the carpenter from Cantwell, Alaska, is helping to man the checkpoint at the finish line because his handlers are travelling with Halvorson's handlers. And none of them had arrived by the time he did.

Fisher is a Quest rookie, running his first long distance race after getting hooked on mushing when he did a friend a favor six years ago and took his small dog team out for a little exercise.

"It's a personal challenge, kind of an ego thing," he says, looking wistfully back down the trail. "It builds confidence in a person. If I can mush a dog team for 1,000 miles, I can do anything."

Then his eyes, a moment before weary and haggard, brighten as he looks beyond the finish line, up the river past where the teams stop, and the Quest blood starts to boil in him again. There is a broken trail, made by a snow machine, wending its way along the edge of the ice, under the bridge that spans the river and around the corner to . . . .

"Is there another town I can run to . . . ? I might as well hitch 'em up."

It is later, as David Monson rides to his hotel, that it gradually seeps in that he is the first and, so far, only finisher of the 1988 Quest — which means he is probably the winner. But there is little peace for him in the first few hours, no time for him to think about what it means and appreciate it.

Even sitting in the bathtub, trying to scrub two weeks of grime and sweat off his body, he is talking to a reporter perched on the lid of the toilet next to him. Finally, he dozes off in the middle of another media interview in his room.

It will be three days before the final banquet. There are teams who will still be on the trail and for those who finish, there is plenty of activity between time spent catching up on long overdue sleep.

The drivers have had plenty of time to look over their opponents' teams during the past two weeks and now is the time to talk trading and selling dogs. The mushers' marketplace is open all year round — it's not unusual to find mushers in midsummer or mid-race wrangling with another musher over a dog or two — but the post-race period is the most frenzied. It is similar to athletes from professional sports franchises being swapped when the season wraps up as teams try to improve for next year.

It takes a while for the dogs and drivers to settle into a normal routine. Like jet-lag or the adjustment a shift-worker has to make, the pattern of run-eat-sleep doesn't just vanish in the one second it takes to complete the race or even with one good night's sleep.

Even something as simple as breathing is an adjustment that has to be made. The warm, more humid air inside a room or building is in sharp contrast to the cold, dry, brittle air they've been inhaling. The driver's sinuses and nostrils, now adapted to a steady diet of outdoor air, react with the indoor air and become constantly plugged, making breathing difficult.

There's nobody to tell the dogs it's over. They've passed under banners, stopped in crowds and been poked, prodded and needled by veterinarians a few times over the past two weeks. To them, this is just another temporary stop, albeit a little more populated than some. The first difference they notice is when they're loaded into their dog boxes and trucked away from the city, to be kenneled on rural lots for the next few days. When they arrive, they curl up motionless on beds of fresh hay for a few hours.

When their internal clock tells them it's time to get up and go, they awake. But there's no one there to take them and no place to go — just a bowl of water, some food and maybe a handler sitting nearby, keeping a careful eye on them. The sled isn't behind them, the tug line and harnesses are gone. There's nothing to pull and no way to pull it if there was.

Confused, they eat and drink, and wait, then lie down and curl up again. Two or three times they repeat that. Eventually they stop waking up and drift into a deep dream-filled sleep. Even then it doesn't end: their legs twitch, their sides heave and they pant. Their imaginations literally run wild.

For the first few days the handler will take the dogs for a jog to loosen them up and take the ache out of their legs. They will welcome the easy jaunt, it tells them that the hard stuff is over for a while. They may get a week or two of easy exercise, then it's back to the racing circuit. The big-money middle distance races are scheduled to be run during the next month. They will greet the reappearance of the sled and harnesses with grins and wagging tails. This is what they were born to. Running is their life.

The drivers also keep waking up, ready to run.

Frank Turner wakes up with a start in the middle of the night: reaching for his boots, wired up with nerves and perspiring heavily, wondering which way his team is facing, who is passing and uncertain of exactly where he is on the trail. And why is the sky so strange. Then he realizes he's in the cabin and the sky is his loft ceiling. There is no sled passing, no trail and the boots in his hand are his bedroom slippers.

Jim Reiter opens his eyes at night and shifts uncomfortably under the covers on his bed. His feet feel strange — instead of being bare, they should be sheathed in mukluks or bunny boots. The blanket feels weird — a parka or sleeping bag would feel more natural. And there's the frustrating feeling of thinking you should be doing something, but you're not sure exactly what.

Jon Rudolph finds that day and night have no meaning.

"It takes me about two weeks to get back into a normal routine, going to bed at night and getting up in the morning. You've been awake all the time. You slept when you could and if you could."

Strange things happen in the twilight zone. Rudolph arrived at the finish line just before two in the morning in '86 and his wife drove him home. On the way he noticed the road to his house had drifted over with snow and thought to himself, "I should plow the road."

The next thing he remembers is waking up five or six hours later in the cab of his grader. But instead of plowing the road, he was 12 miles away heading down the highway into Whitehorse.

"What the hell am I doing here?" he asked himself, "Taking a grader downtown?" He turned around, returned home and plowed off his driveway before returning to bed.

"I was able to run the kind of race I wanted to at the end — it paid off for me. I was really happy," Dave Monson says in his victory speech at the mushers' banquet. "To me the Yukon Quest is a spirit of adventure, of travel through some of the prettiest country in the northern latitudes . . . certainly, in its own respect, the prettiest in the world.

It's about camaraderie and companionship, competition, loneliness, hardship and pain, the will to persevere and succeed.

It's all these things rolled into one.

It's the musher and dogs in companionship against the elements and the teamwork between the two that helps you overcome the obstacles and make your goal."

At the banquet, he basks in the public's adulation and hero worship for the newly crowned champion.

But later, in his bed that night, it is a good feeling being alone. In the solitude, he savours his accomplishment. He is proud of his dogs. He is at peace within himself.

THE DOGS

The little dogs had the hardest of times getting over the long, long trail. The trail is a very rough trail to get over.

When your little dog finishes the QUEST what do you do to it? Do you thank it? I think it is hard on the dogs and you don't know what it would be like to be the dogs. I think that all your dogs need a lot of credit for pulling you and your things over the finish line.

I know that the first person over the finish line gets a trophy and 20,000 dollars, but think of your dogs. Don't forget to thank your dogs. They did most of the work.

By Erin Briemon

Erin Briemon is an 11-year resident of Whitehorse who likes to watch the Yukon Quest, either in Whitehorse or on Lake Laberge, especially the dogs.

SLEDOG RACING

That's how it is spelled in Europe — Sledog Racing — with one "d."

Not only is the spelling different, so is the way the Europeans approach the sport of dog driving. The checkpoints and start and finish areas are like a carnival: bright, colourful and noisy. Military bands greet or send off the teams. Dining is gourmet food and fine wines. Accommodation is four-star hotels. And the people . . . thousands flock to see the dogs, from crowds of 10,000 at small regional sprint meets to teeming masses in excess of 50,000 per day lining the route of the Alpirod.

"In Alaska we're not used to seeing a lot of people. It's wilderness and forests of trees," says Joe Runyan, winner of the 1988 Alpirod, "In Europe, there are forests of people and the trees are rare. It's really very confusing for the dogs every once in a while." Runyan is the only musher to have won all three of the world's long distance sled dog races — The 1985 Yukon Quest, the 1988 Alpirod and the 1989 Iditarod.

To actually drive dogs in Europe is expensive. Teams must be flown over from Alaska at great cost; teams based in Europe are owned by those who can afford it. With the exception of the Alpirod, there are no cash prizes for the drivers and professionals are unheard of. Despite the lack of cash prizes, the Alaskans like coming to Europe. Success here can spell large endorsement contracts with outdoor equipment manufacturers — a trend which is just starting to reap limited rewards for the Americans in their own country.

In Europe, dog driving is a sport only for the wealthy: buying and maintaining a team is an expensive pastime. It is no wonder then that it was only a small select group that kept the sport barely alive until the last decade. Not many of European aristocracy and society wanted to be seen in the company of a bunch of dogs. But times change, as do the views of what is socially acceptable and what isn't.

Now it's a rapidly growing activity. New sledog racing clubs are being formed virtually every six months. The number of regional races had grown from two or three per country in the mid-1970s to eight or 10 by the early '80s.

There are national championships, and European championships which attract up to 300 teams from Germany, France, Switzerland, Austria and northern Italy.

The Alpirod, a four-country 1000-mile event, was the brainchild of Armen Khatchikian, an Italian who got hooked on sledog racing when he won a national "What is Your Desire?" contest in his home country. His desire was to run the Iditarod, and that's what he did with the $50,000 in prize money.

When he returned home, he set about organizing a major European long distance race and in 1988 his dream came true.

Joe Runyan beat 25 other teams to the finish line in the 10-day event, including four-time Iditarod champion Rick Swenson and the first woman to ever win the Iditarod, Libby Riddles.

In 1989, it was Kathy Swenson's turn to step into the winner's circle. With Libby Riddles and Susan Butcher winning the Iditarod, of the three major long distance races in the world, only the Yukon Quest still waits for a female champion.

The Alaskans are still the cream of the world mushing family, but the Europeans are starting to make major progress towards that domination. Those Europeans, like Switzerland's Martin Buser and France's Tony Andreone, originally got started into mushing while in Alaska and have acquired most of their experience and training in North America.

Interest in dog mushing around the world has been high enough over the years that it was actually a recognized demonstration sport in the 1932 Lake Placid Winter Olympics. Canada's Emile St. Godard won the gold, edging out American driving legend Leonhard Seppala.

In 1988, the Alberta International Sled Dog Classic was held as a demonstration for the International Olympic Committee just two weeks before the Olympic Games in Calgary, Alberta. Over 170 teams from nine countries took part in the three day event, held in the hopes of earning Olympic support to reinstate the sport as an official event.

Wherever there are winter wonderlands, there are sled dog clubs. Canada, a country covered by snow over 90 per cent of its area for almost 50 per cent of each year, is riddled with them from the mountains of the north, to the plains of the central provinces, through the lakes of Ontario and onto the rocky shores of the Maritimes.

The northeastern United States — Maine, New York, Vermont, New Hampshire and New England — have a history of using dog sleds going back to the early nineteenth century and have had an organized racing circuit since 1922. Across the northern central states, middle distance racing, like Minnesota's John Beargrease 400, are popular. And in the far west, dog drivers can be found racing in northern California, Arizona, Oregon, Washington and Utah.

Even where there are no snowdrifts, but sand dunes instead, mushers run dogs pulling sleds on rubber tires.

Terry Quesnel was a veterinarian for the 1987 Yukon Quest and one of the organizers behind the 1988 races for the Olympic community before the Calgary Olympics.

"It's an elegant sport," he says, "With lots of romance and history to it."

Even when they're not being used in a sport, dog teams are invaluable. They have been used extensively in both Arctic and Antarctic exploration. At one time, in Nome, Alaska, they were even used to pull a railway train when no engine could be imported.

Somewhere in the world, at any given moment, a driver is hitching up his or her team. He or she may "hike" their dogs with a southern drawl, the clipped perfection of the Queen's English, the rolling brogue of a Scotsman, the structured formality of German, the romantic flow of French, the emotion of Italian or the casual tones of the Alaskan driver.

Individually, they are as different from one another as thousands of individual people can be. But when they step on those runners, something happens that transcends all the cultural, political and personal boundaries. They all seek the same fantasy: adventure, glory and wealth.

226

RACE RESULTS

1984

Place	Musher	Time	Money
1	Sonny Lindner, Johnson River, Alaska	12:00:05	$15,000
2	Harry Sutherland, Johnson River, Alaska	12:04:15	10,000
3	Bill Cotter, Nenana, Alaska	12:05:40	5,000
4	Joe Runyan, Tanana, Alaska	12:07:51	4,400
5	Jeff King, Denali Park, Alaska	12:10:59	3,300
6	Bruce Johnson, Atlin, British Columbia	12:18:07	2,400
7	Gerald Riley, Nenana, Alaska	12:21:58	1,900
8	Jack Hayden, Lake Minchumina, Alaska	12:22:40	1,500
9	Kevin Turnbough, Grand Marais, Minnesota	12:23:12	1,400
10	Pecos Humphreys, Talkeetna, Alaska	13:03:07	1,000
11	Lorrina Mitchell, Whitehorse, Yukon	13:03:08	900
12	Senley Yuill, Whitehorse, Yukon	13:03:08	800
13	Ron Aldrich, Montana Creek, Alaska	13:12:48	700
14	Frank Turner, Pelly Crossing, Yukon	13:20:37	600
15	Wilson Sam, Huslia, Alaska	13:20:38	500
16	Mary Sheilds, Schimmelpfenning Creek	14:17:19	
17	Murray Clayton, Haines, Alaska	14:17:23	
18	Don Glassburn, Central, Alaska	14:23:55	
19	Nick Ericson, Fairbanks, Alaska	15:08:11	
20	Shirley Liss, Fairbanks, Alaska	*Finished at Carmacks due to poor trail.*	

Official scratches
Chris Whaley, John Two Rivers, Dave Klumb, Daryle Adkins, Jack Stevens, Bob English

1985

Place	Musher	Time	Money
1	Joe Runyan, Tanana, Alask	11:11:55	$15,000
2	Rick Atkinson, Scotland	11:12:15	10,000
3	Harry Sutherland, Johnson River, Alaska	11:13:25	5,800
4	Jeff King, Denali Park, Alaska	11:14:31	4,400
5	Bill Cotter, Nenana, Alaska	11:15:23	3,300
6	Dennis Kogl, Denali Park, Alaska	12:02:31	2,400

7	Walter Kaso, Talkeetna, Alaska	12:04:55	1,900
8	Bruce Johnson, Atlin, B.C.	12:05:41	1,500
9	Joe May Trapper Creek, Alaska	12:06:05	1,200
10	Jack Hayden Lake Minchumina, Alaska	12:06:06	1,000
11	Jon Gleason, Fairbanks, Alaska	12:08:15	900
12	Rick Dunlap, Fairbanks, Alaska	12:12:06	800
13	Murray Clayton, Haines, Alaska	12:15:39	700
14	Jon Rudolph, Whitehorse, Yukon	12:16:37	600
15	Eric Buetow, Two Rivers, Alaska	12:16:50	500
16	Frank Turner, Pelly Crossing, Yukon	12:22:08	
17	Nick Ericson, Fairbanks, Alaska	12:23:07	
18	Patricia Doval, College, Alaska	13:16:10	
19	Connie Frerichs, Delta Junction, Alaska	13:17:11	
20	Julie Collins, Lake Minchumina, Alaska	13:18:50	
21	Ron Rosser, Pleasant Valley, Alaska	14:02:00	
22	Frank Ganley, Fairbanks, Alaska	14:07:43	
23	John Mitchell, Dawson City, Yukon	14:22:00	
24	Pete Bowers, Goldstream, Alaska	15:02:32	
25	Jim Bennett, Fairbanks, Alaska	15:07:03	
26	Stan Bearup, Fairbanks, Alaska	15:17:59	
27	Shirley Liss, Fairbanks, Alaska	18:10:28	
28	Jim Bridges, Knik, Alaska	18:14:17	

Official Scratches
Richard Hayden, Lena Charley, Don Honea, Gerald Riley, Russ Ridlington,
Glenn Craig

1986

Place	Musher	Time	Money
1	Bruce Johnson , Atlin, B.C.	14:09:17	$15,000
2	Jeff King, Denali Park, Alaska	14:09:41	10,000
3	Tim Osmar, Clam Gulch, Alaska	14:10:21	5,000
4	Sonny Lindner, Johnson River, Alaska	14:10:48	4,400
5	Harry Sutherland, Johnson River, Alaska	14:11:01	3,300
6	Bill Cotter, Nenana, Alaska	14:11:50	2,400
7	Ed Foran, Nenana, Alaska	14:11:52	1,900
8	John Schandelmeier, McLaren Creek, Alaska	14:12:23	1,500
9	Joe May, Trapper Creek, Alaska	14:13:23	1,200
10	Jon Rudolph, Whitehorse, Yukon	14:13:53	1,000
11	Mary Sheilds, Schemmelpfenning Creek	14:14:59	900
12	Bruce Lee, Denali Park, Alaska	14:16:41	800
13	Martin Weiner, Denali Park, Alaska	14:18:46	700
14	Tony Andreonne, France	14:19:57	600
15	Don Glassburn, Central, Alaska	14:20:21	500

16	Francois Varigas, France	14:20:21
17	Kathy Swenson, Manley, Alaska	15:01:06
18	Adolphus Capot-Blanc, Fort Nelson, B.C.	15:01:50
19	Frank Ganley, Fairbanks, Alaska	15:03:49
20	Lena Charley, Christochena, Alaska	15:22:50
21	Cor Guimond, Dawson City, Yukon	15:23:27
22	Bill Fliris, Tanana, Alaska	16:06:06
23	Dean Seibold, Delta Junction, Alaska	16:06:46
24	Ron Rosser, Pleasant Valley,Alaska	16:11:50
25	Ralph Tingey, Denali Park, Alaska	16:12:05
26	Michael Schwandt, Soldotna, Alaska	19:02:19

Official Scratches
Connie Frerichs, Frank Turner, Ed Borden, Floyd Terry, Rob Weathers, Arthur Church, Bur Lydic, Frank Robbins, Robin Jacobsen, Jim Bridges, Dave Schmitz, David Likins

1987

Place	Musher	Time	Money
1	Bill Cotter, Nenana, Alaska	12:04:34	$15,000
2	David Monson, Manley, Alaska	12:04:44	10,000
3	Jeff King, Denali Park, Alaska	12:04:52	5,000
4	Kathy Swenson, Manley, Alaska	12:05:10	4,400
5	Rick Atkinson, Scotland	12:06:25	3,300
6	John Schandlemeier, Paxson, Alaska	12:22:16	2,400
7	Francois Varigas, Dawson City, Yukon	13:04:29	1,900
8	Ed Salter, Manley, Alaska	13:05:12	1,500
9	Marc Boily, Nome, Alaska	13:07:09	1,200
10	Dean Seibold, Delta Junction, Alaska	13:08:30	1,000
11	Ralph Tingey, Denali Park, Alaska	13:08:37	900
12	Susan Whiton, Trapper Creek, Alaska	13:16:01	800
13	Larry Johnson, Nenana, Alaska	13:22:48	700
14	David Sawatzky, Healy, Alaska	14:03:49	600
15	Kevin Turnbough, Fairbanks, Alaska	14:08:03	500
16	Jim Wardlow, Delta Junction, Alaska	14:10:07	
17	Karin Schmidt, North Pole, Alaska	14:18:18	
18	Connie Frerichs, Delta Junction, Alaska	15:03:57	
19	Don Donaldson, Delta Junction, Alaska	15:08:22	
20	LeRoy Shank, Fairbanks, Alaska	15:12:12	
21	Allen Dennis, Salcha, Alaska	15:15:47	

Official Scratches
Rob Weathers, Craig Wolter, Ty Duggar, Kelly Wages, Hans Oettli, Larry Grout, Jim Reiter, Vince Stack, Lorrina Mitchell, Pecos Humphries, Frank Turner, Don Glassburn, Jon Gleason
Official Disqualifications
Floyd Terry, Larry Hand, Mark Grober, Lolly Medley, Kathy Tucker

1988

Place	Musher	Time	Money
1	David Monson, Manley, Alaska	12:05:06	$20,000
2	Gerald Riley, Nenana, Alaska	12:14:01	15,000
3	Kathy Swenson, Fairbanks, Alaska	12:16:14	10,000
4	Rick Atkinson, Bettles, Alaska	13:01:38	7,000
5	Bruce Lee, Denali Park, Alaska	13:04:22	5,000
6	Kate Persons, Kotzebue, Alaska	13:15:02	3,500
7	John Schandlmeier, Paxson, Alaska	13:15:24	2,800
8	Dennis Kogl, Denali Park, Alaska	13:18:53	2,250
9	Ralph Tingey, Denali Park, Alaska	13:21:06	1,950
10	Jim Wardlow, Delta Junction, Alaska	13:23:13	1,750
11	Vern Halter, Trapper Creek, Alaska	14:03:28	1,550
12	Frank Turner, Pelly Crossing, Yukon	14:12:15	1,350
13	Mark Elliot, Dawson City, Yukon	14:13:31	1,150
14	Lorrina Mitchell, Whitehorse, Yukon	14:16:58	950
15	Frank Ganley, Fairbanks, Alaska	14:17:09	750
16	Mary Sheilds, Schemmelpfenning Creek	14:17:15	
17	Ron Rosser, Fort Yukon, Alaska	15:05:26	
18	Mark Stamm, Bothel, Washington	15:05:29	
19	Ned Cathers, Whitehorse, Yukon	15:09:42	
20	Lena Charley, Gakona, Alaska	15:20:16	
21	Dave Dalton, Fairbanks, Alaska	15:23:01	
22	Jim Strong, Hope, Alaska	16:01:50	
23	Bob Holder, Fairbanks, Alaska	16:02:12	
24	Jim Reiter, Central, Alaska	17:13:29	
25	Jeff Fisher, Cantwell, Alaska	17:14:13	
26	Tom Randall, Whitehorse, Yukon	17:14:40	
27	James Poage, Central, Alaska	19:02:57	
28	Marc Poage, Central, Alaska	19:07:43	
29	John Ballard, Salcha, Alaska	20:06:26	
30	Ty Halvorson, North Pole, Alaska	20:09:16	

Official Scratches
Jeff King, Scott Poage, Steve Mullen, Francois Varigas, Don Donaldson, Ben LeFebvre, Jim Bennett, Steve Haver, Adolphus Capot-Blanc, Allen Dennis, Dick Barnum, Larry Smith, Mike Kramer, Bob Bright, David Sawatzky, Jon Gleason

1989

Place	Musher	Time	Money
1	Jeff King, Denali Park, Alaska,	11:20:51	$20,000
2	Vern Halter, Trapper Creek, Alaska	11:21:11	15,000
3	Jim Wilson, Kobuk, Alaska	11:21:56	10,000
4	Bruce Lee, Denali Park, Alaska	11:23:35	7,000

5	Kate Persons, Kotzebue, Alaska	12:00:29	5,000
6	Sonny Lindner, Fairbanks, Alaska	12:00:39	3,500
7	Francois Varigas, Dawson City, Yukon	12:02:36	2,800
8	Linda Forsberg, Denali Park, Alaska	13:03:06	2,250
9	Kathy Tucker, Manley, Alaska	13:03:08	1,950
10	Frank Turner, Pelly Crossing, Yukon	13:04:28	1,750
11	Charlie Boulding, Nenana, Alaska	13:04:52	1,550
12	Nick Ericson, Fairbanks, Alaska	13:05:40	1,350
13	Fred Jordan, Tanana, Alaska	13:06:17	1,150
14	Harry Sutherland, Johnson River, Alaska	13:08:21	950
15	Ned Cathers, Whitehorse, Yukon	13:11:05	750
16	David Sawatzky, Healy, Alaska	13:11:14	
17	Larry Smith, Dawson City, Yukon	14:01:06	
18	David Scheer, Kasilof, Alaska	14:04:47	
19	Heath Duncan, Soldotna, Alaska	14:06:27	
20	Bob Holder, Fairbanks, Alaska	14:08:42	
21	Ketil Reitan, Norway	14:09:52	
22	Mike Maurer, Salcha, Alaska	14:09:55	
23	Ralph Seekins, Fairbanks, Alaska	14:14:47	
24	Steve Barb, Healy, Alaska	14:19:07	
25	John Anderson, Willow, Alaska	15:03:19	
26	Dick Barnum, Fairbanks, Alaska	15:04:41	
27	Jennine Cathers, Whitehorse, Yukon	15:13:13	
28	Scott Cameron, Palmer, Alaska	15:17:21	
29	Jeff Fisher, Cantwell, Alaska	15:17:49	
30	Charles Gauthier, Faro, Yukon	16:01:21	
31	Peter Butteri, Tok, Alaska	16:23:34	

Official Scratches
Charlotte Fitzhugh, Bob Grawher, Bob Bright, Bob Pelling, Brian MacDougall, James Poage, Kris Krestensen, Tom Randall, Marc Poage, Dennis Schmidt, Amy Squibb

Official Disqualifications
Steve Mullen, Larry Johnson, Gerald Riley

1990

Place	Musher	Time	Money
1	Vern Halter, Trapper Creek, Alaska	11:17:09	$20,000
2	Jeff King, Denali Park, Alaska	11:19:33	15,000
3	Francois Varigas, Dawson City, Yukon	11:23:32	10,000
4	Kate Persons, Kotzebue, Alaska	12:01:05	7,000
5	Linda Forsberg, Denali Park, Alaska	12:10:16	5,000
6	Peter Thomann, Switzerland	12:14:27	3,500
7	Darwin McLeod	12:14:31	2,800
8	Dave Sawatzky, Healy, Alaska	12:16:30	2,250

9	Will Forsberg, Denali Park, Alaska	12:18:30	1,950
10	Charlie Boulding, Nenana, Alaska	12:19:36	1,750
11	Ned Cathers, Whitehorse, Yukon	12:20:25	1,550
12	John Schandelmeier, Paxson, Alaska	12:22:16	1,350
13	Larry Smith, Dawson City, Yukon	13:02:22	1,150
14	Tim Mowrey, Fairbanks, Alaska	13:09:05	950
15	Marc Poage, Central, Alaska	13:13:54	750
16	Dave Dalton, Fairbanks, Alaska	13:15:03	
17	William Kleedehn, Kenora, Ontario	13:16:16	
18	Jennine Cathers, Whitehorse, Yukon	14:00:41	
19	Frank Turner, Pelly Crossing, Yukon	14:01:04	
20	Rick Wintter, Fairbanks, Alaska	15:20:52	
21	Terri Frerichs, Delta Junction, Alaska	15:21:02	
22	Paul Taylor, Fairbanks, Alaska	15:21:13	
23	Connie Frerichs, Delta Junction, Alaska	15:21:28	
24	Bob Holder, Fairbanks, Alaska	15:21:47	
25	Jim Reiter, Central, Alaska	15:22:39	
26	Esa Ekdahl, Whitehorse, Yukon	16:10:03	

Official Scratches
Peter Butteri, Hans Oettli, Gary Moore, Knowland Silas, Becky Sather, LeRoy Shank, Brian Lawson, Mark Elliot, Phil Cole, Adolphus Capot-Blanc

Official Disqualifications
Michael Maurer

FIFTH ANNUAL YUKON QUEST SLED DOG RACE

Official Race Rules for the 1988 Yukon Quest
International Sled Dog Race

General Race Procedure

1. Race Start:

The official starting date for the 1988 race will be February 20, 1988 at 11:00 a.m. local time. Official starting place will be Fairbanks, Alaska, unless otherwise designated by Yukon Quest International (hereinafter referred to as YQI). The race will be held as scheduled regardless of weather conditions. Each year the starting date and time will be determined by YQI. In odd numbered years the race will start in Whitehorse, Yukon Territory, and in even numbered years the race will start in Fairbanks, Alaska. The starting place may be changed by the Race Marshal and judges because of weather and/or trail conditions.

2. Entry Fee:

Receipt of the entry fee and form will constitute the musher's intent to enter the race and further acknowledges that the musher understands and agrees to comply with each and every rule as stated. Entries will be limited to the first fifty (50) mushers. The entry fee will be Six Hundred Fifty Dollars ($650.00) U.S. currency to be delivered to YQI in person or by certified mail by midnight, January 1, 1988. Entries received or postmarked between January 1 and midnight, January 22, 1988 may be accepted at a fee of Eight hundred Fifty Dollars ($850.00). All entries must be accompanied by a completed official YQI entry form. Kennel entries will be allowed. The driver must be named by midnight January 1, 1988. Driver substitutions necessitated by medical reasons will be permitted up to the mushers' meeting, upon approval of the Rules Committee of YQI. The dates may change at the discretion of YQI and YQI reserves the right to reject any and all entries. *The entry fee for any entrant withdrawing after January 1, 1988 will not be refunded.*

3. Course and Checkpoints:

The course covers approximately 1,000 miles of mostly Arctic wilderness, much of it on and along the Yukon River. The trail will be broken and marked prior to the race, but due to weather conditions there will be no guarantee of broken trail during the race. (A map and compass are required equipment.) Major checkpoints are as follows:

1. Fairbanks
2. Angel Creek
3. Central
4. Circle Hot Springs
5. Circle City
6. Eagle
7. Dawson
8. Carmacks
9. Whitehorse

4. Food / Equipment Shipment:

All foods and equipment shipments must be in Cloth Burlap Bags. Gross weight not to exceed 60 pounds. Bags must be turned into YQI prior to food shipment deadline or delivered to checkpoint prior to start of race. No food or equipment will be delivered to checkpoints after start of race with the exception of Dawson.

The following amounts of dog food are suggested. If a musher obtains dog food between checkpoints, that musher may be penalized or disqualified.

Fairbanks	- 5 pounds per dog	Eagle	-10 pounds per dog
Angel Creek	-10 pounds per dog	Dawson	-30 pounds per dog
Circle Hot Springs	-10 pounds per dog	Carmacks	-15 pounds per dog
Circle City	-15 pounds per dog		

5. Promotional Material:
YQI may require a small amount of promotional freight as part of the mandatory load. Promotional material must be turned in to race official at completion of race or when scratching.

6. Shipping Dropped Dogs:
Mushers will pay for all transportation expenses incurred or relevant to the return of their dropped dogs. YQI will supervise transportation of dogs from "Fly In Only" checkpoints. Transportation for dogs dropped at other checkpoints (along the road system) may be arranged for by the musher, or will be provided by YQI at the musher's expense.

7. Race Officials:
The Race Marshall or judges in conjunction with a veterinarian will have absolute authority over the dog teams. Their judgment as to withdrawal of a dog or dogs from the race or any other conditions relative to dog care on the trail shall be final.

8. Vet Check:
All dogs will undergo a physical examination before the race starts. Examinations will be performed by licensed veterinarians. Any dog that cannot qualify for a certificate of good health may not run in the race. All examinations must be done within ten (10) days prior to the start of the race. All dogs entered in the race will have current parvo, rabies, and distemper shots. Rabies vaccinations must come from a licensed veterinarian or certified technician. Proof or vaccination for rabies, distemper and parvo must be presented to the official veterinarian at the time of the Vet Check on the scheduled day of the Vet Check. The musher must present the team or proof of previous examination to the official veterinarian at the Vet Check. Failure to comply will result in disqualification. The time and place of the Vet Check will be announced by YQI.

9. Mushers' Meeting and Drawing:
It will be mandatory for all entrants to attend a mushers' meeting immediately prior to the mushers' banquet. Failure to answer all roll calls in person will result in disqualification. The time and place for this meeting will be announced by YQI. Each musher must draw his starting position in person at the banquet.

10. Prize Money:

1. $20,000	6. $3,500	11. $1,550
2. $15,000	7. $2,800	12. $1,350
3. $10,000	8. $2,250	13. $1,150
4. $ 7,000	9. $1,950	14. $ 950
5. $ 5,000	10. $1,750	15. $ 750

In the event that less than $75,000 is raised for prize money, the awards will be paid on a percentage basis of prize money available in relation to $75,000.

11. Sled:
Only one (1) sled per musher will be used throughout the race. Each musher has a choice of his own sled, subject to the condition that some kind of sled or toboggan must be drawn. The sled or toboggan must be capable of hauling any injured or fatigued dogs and the required food, materials, and equipment. In the event of repair, the sled must not be altered significantly as to weight or size. Incidental help with sled repairs is allowed.

12. Awards Presentation:
The awards presentation ceremony at Whitehorse/Fairbanks will be held the evening following seventy-two (72) hours after the first team crosses the finish line. All mushers who have crossed the finish line up to two (2) hours before the ceremony will be present and the winner will have a representative of his dog team present for recognition. An official finish is a prerequisite for receiving any awards. Those who do not attend the awards presentation ceremony may be fined up to Five Hundred Dollars ($500.00).

13. Claims:
Each musher agrees to hold YQI, the race sponser(s) and other contributors (that is, sponsors and contributors of the race corporation as distinguished from the sponsors of individual mushers) harmless from any claim or demand based on any alleged action or inaction by the musher, his dogs, agents or others acting in his behalf, The musher also agrees to release YQI, race sponser(s), and their agents and employees from any claim or demand resulting from injury to the musher, his dogs, or his property. Further, YQI has the unqualified and unrestricted authority to authorize the race sponser(s) to photograph and otherwise collect information for advertising, public relations or other publicity purposes,. Each musher shall sign any and all documents as may be requested by YQI. These documents will be executed prior to or at the mushers' meeting. Any musher who does mot sign the documents requested by YQI will not be allowed to participate in the race.

14. Protest:
To be recognized as a legitimate protest, any infraction observed by a musher must be protested in writing on official forms at the next checkpoint.

15. Censure:
In reference to action taken by race officials or the race, the Board of Directors after the race, the Board of Directors of YQI may censure a musher for cause, including prohibition from entering future race or races. The musher so involved may request in writing an informal hearing before a mutually agreeable arbitration board within thirty (30) days of the date of censure.

16. Failure To Adhere:
Failure to adhere to the published Rules of General Race and Trail Procedure and policy will allow race officials to disqualify a musher or to impose a monetary or time penalty. In the event fines are imposed, any future application will not be accepted until full payment is received by YQI. Disqualified mushers will forfeit all placements and monetary values.

TRAIL PROCEDURE

1. Common Start/Late Start:
For elapsed time purposes the race will be a common start event. Each musher's elapsed time between Fairbanks and Whitehorse will be calculated using 11:00 a.m. on February 20, 1988 as the starting time. Any musher who cannot leave the starting line in order drawn, will be started after the musher who drew last place has left. Any team that cannot leave the starting line within sixty (60) minutes of the last team's departure may be disqualified. Common start event means that although teams will leave the starting line at two (2) minute intervals, each team's official starting time will be regarded as 11:00 a.m. Make-up time will be clarified in Rule 3.

2. Check-in/Sign-out:
Every musher must personally check in and sign out at each major checkpoint before going on. A musher is not officially checked in until he has all the required gear. If a musher loses a required article of gear between checkpoints, he cannot check in at the next checkpoint until he has acquired and replaced the lost item. Except for start and finish, major checkpoints are Angel Creek, Central, Circle Hot Springs, Circle City, Eagle, Dawson, and Carmacks.

3. 36 Hour Stop (Dawson):
One mandatory thirty-six (36) hour stop at Dawson, Yukon Territory, will be required during the running of the race. Time begins when the driver checks in at Dawson. The starting time differential will be compensated for during each team's mandatory thirty-six (36) hour layover so that each team has equal trail time. YQI will give each musher the required time information prior to his leaving the starting line. The Following Is Allowed In Dawson: (a) Food and equipment can be delivered after start of race; (b) Assistance with feeding dogs and repairing equipment. THE FOLLOWING IS NOT ALLOWED IN DAWSON: (a) Removing dogs from holding area; (b) Housing dogs in dog boxes or autos and trucks.

16. Substitutes:
Once a musher leaves the starting line, no substitutes will be permitted to replace him.

17. Treatment of Dogs:
There will be no cruel or inhumane treatment of dogs. Race veterinarians shall have final authority to remove a dog from the race for medical reasons.

18. Tampering:
No musher may tamper with another musher's dogs, food or gear. Requested help is not "tampering".

19. Withdrawal from the Race:
Mushers wishing to withdraw from the race may scratch at official checkpoints only. To scratch, the musher must fill out and sign an official scratch form which will indicate his wishes concerning his supplies at subsequent checkpoints, his travel plans and his reason for scratching. Items remaining from supplies received by a musher at prior checkpoints will become the responsibility and therefore the property of YQI. YQI will in no way be responsible for supplies at subsequent checkpoints for mushers who scratch or are disqualified. Frontier courtesy, however, will prevail.

20. Motorized Vehicles:
In no case may a musher accept assistance from any type of motorized vehicle between checkpoints.

21. Pacing:
Pacing will not be permitted.

22. Killing of Game Animals:
In the event that an edible game animal, i.e. moose, caribou, buffalo, is killed in defense of life or property, the musher must take measures to salvage the meat for human use and report the incident at the next checkpoint. This means that a food animal must be gutted, then reported at the next checkpoint. YQI will make arrangements for further salvage. Any other animal killed in defense of life or property should be reported.

23. Mandatory Gear:
Each musher must have in his possession at all times the following items:

1. Proper cold weather sleeping bag.
2. Hand ax with an overall length of at least 22".
3. One pair of snowshoes at least 35" long and 7" wide with bindings.
4. Any promotional material that the musher has been asked to carry to Fairbanks/ Whitehorse by YQI.
5. Map and compass.

In addition eight (8) booties for each dog, either in the sled or in use and in the sled, are required when a musher signs out of checkpoint.

Mushers should have these items in their possession at all times. However, in the event of accidental or unavoidable loss along the trail, the musher will be allowed to replace the missing item(s) at the next checkpoint before checking in.

24. Dropped Dogs:
Any injured, fatigued or sick dogs may be dropped at checkpoints without penalty. Each dropped dog must be left with two days' food and a reliable chain or cable. Mushers are responsible for providing the chain or the cable, collar, and proper amounts of food for dropped dogs. A minimum amount of food is two pounds per day per dog.

A dog may be dropped for emergency medical reasons between checkpoints. The musher will assume responsibility for the care of that dog and all fees incurred. This action must be reported to the race officials at the next checkpoint and the musher may be subject to penalties. The dog must be examined by a race veterinarian and accounted for prior to the start of the Awards Banquet.

25. Expired Dogs:
Any dog that expires on the trail for any reason must be taken to the next checkpoint or checkpoint just passed, and submitted to race official. A necropsy will be performed on all expired dogs by a licensed veterinary pathologist or veterinarian.

26. Demand for Food and Shelter:
A musher may not make demands for food or shelter along the trail or at checkpoints.

27. Hotels and Lodges:
Sleeping areas will be designated at each checkpoint.

28. Care and Feeding of Dogs:
No planned help is allowed throughout the race with the exception of Dawson. All care and feeding of dogs will be done by the mushers only. Mushers may assist one another between checkpoints. At non-checkpoints, a musher may accept hospitality for himself only.

29. Hauling Dogs:
A musher may not allow any of his dogs to be hauled by another team. A musher's dogs hauled in his own sled must be hauled in a protected, humane manner.

30. Unmanageable Team:
Outside assistance will be allowed only if a team is unmanageable. Whether a team is unmanageable will be ruled upon by the Race Marshall in each separate instance.

31. Loose Leaders:
There will be no loose leaders; all dogs will be in the team or on the sled. A musher must immediately make every effort to secure any dog which accidentally becomes loose.

32. Lost Team:
In the case of a lost team, the team will not be disqualified if the driver regains control of the team, provided that the team and driver complete the entire race trail and comply with the rules including checkpoint requirements. As long as the team and driver continue on the trail when separated, the driver may continue on when regaining control. A musher may receive assistance from another musher in recovering his team. All teams must follow the trail as marked or instructed by officials.

33. Drugs:
No injectable, oral, or topical drugs which may suppress the signs of illness or injury to the dogs may be carried or used by the musher. YQI race veterinarians shall have the authority to collect blood or urine samples at random at any point prior to the race, commencing at the official vet check, and at any time after the official starting of the race. Veterinarians have the authority to collect blood and/or urine samples immediately after the finish of each team in Fairbanks. It will be the musher's responsibility to assist the race veterinarian in collection of these samples at the check, during the race and immediately following the team's finish in Fairbanks.

The following drugs are prohibited:
1. Analgesics (pain relievers), prescriptive or non-prescriptive.
2. Anti-inflammatory drugs including corticosteroids, anti-prostaglandins, sali cylates, and DMSO. The exception to this rule will be the use of topical foot medications containing steroids and/or DMSO.
3. Nervous system stimulants.
4. Cough suppressants.
5. Diuretics.
6. Muscle relaxants.
7. Antihistamines.
8. Diet pills

The following drugs will be permitted subject to the approval of a race veterinarian at the Vet Check:

1. Topical medications
2. Aspirin
3. Antibiotics
4. Antidiarrheals

Race veterinarians must be notified of any dogs receiving drugs prescribed to treat an existing medical problem. A statement from the attending veterinarian describing the diagnosis and treatment will be required at the Vet Check.

No drugs or other artificial means may be used to drive a dog beyond his natural ability. A musher must have his team free of any prohibited drugs at the time of the vet check and during the race. If a race veterinarian finds it necessary to use one of these drugs or means for the dog's well being, that dog must be dropped from the race.

34. Finish:
An official finish shall be determined when the nose of the dog in lead crosses the finish line. If a musher finishes the race missing any mandatory gear, thirty (30) minutes per item will be added to the finish time.

35. Statutory Compliance:
Any musher who, while in the race, violates a state, territorial, national or international law (including export-import laws pertaining to firearms) will be disqualified if convicted.

36. Sportsmanship:
The code of the North dictates that all travelers be courteous, helpful, generous and honorable to a degree that will inspire and ensure enduring concern for their welfare in the minds of their hosts. Conduct yourself well enough so that the next musher will be welcomed with equal hospitality.

Any competitor or athlete worthy of the name realizes that all people-officials, volunteers, media, and fans-are equally participants in this event and that it is the musher's responsibility to define the upper limits of human performance. A true Sportsman is an inspiration to all witnesses.

For further information on Yukon Quest, please contact:

Yukon Quest International
P.O. Box 5555
Whitehorse, Yukon
Y1A 1C5
Phone: (403) 667-2144

Yukon Quest International
P.O. Box 75015
Fairbanks, Alaska
99707
Phone: (907) 452-7954

ABOUT THE AUTHOR

A lifelong resident of the Yukon, John Firth has worked as a prospector, an expeditor, journalist, public relations director and theatre manager. He is currently a financial planning agent representing the Mutual Group. Writing is his hobby. This is his first book. Long distance running is his sport. He does not mush dogs.

Printed in Canada